EXPOSITORY PREACHING
FOR TODAY

Andrew Watterson Blackwood

EXPOSITORY PREACHING FOR TODAY

CASE STUDIES OF BIBLE PASSAGES

BAKER BOOK HOUSE
Grand Rapids, Michigan

© 1943 by Pierce & Washabaugh
Library of Congress Catalog Card
Number: 53-5392
ISBN: 0-8010-0639-2

Paperback Edition
issued July 1975 by
Baker Book House
with permission of copyright owner

First printing, July 1975
Second printing, August 1977

Library of Congress Catalog Card Number: 53-5392

PHOTOLITHOPRINTED BY CUSHING - MALLOY, INC.
ANN ARBOR, MICHIGAN, UNITED STATES OF AMERICA
1977

DEDICATED TO THE

PASTOR

*Who Enjoys Preaching from
the Bible*

FOREWORD

LOCAL PASTORS AND SEMINARY PROFESSORS, AS WELL AS divinity students, have been asking me to prepare a book about expository preaching for today. At ministerial conferences and by mail these friends have been appealing for a practical guidebook. They call attention to the scarcity of literature on the subject, especially since some of the better works have gone out of print. These advisers believe in other sorts of pulpit work, and so do I. Still they sense the need today for expository food, well cooked and served warm. They think about meeting the needs of men, and not merely about explaining something from the past. Such friends have led me to deal with a subject full of difficulty, and also full of fascination.

These requests appeal to me strongly for many reasons, not least because my volunteer advisers have never led me astray. Indirectly they have led to each of my books for ministers, all of them still on the active list. The requests also accord with my own experience as a teaching pastor for seventeen years, and as a practical teacher ever since. Throughout this book I have in view two sorts of readers: the pastor who wishes to prepare expository messages for today, and the student who thinks more in terms of tomorrow. In either case I should feel sorry if anyone used the volume simply as a storehouse full of food for the sheep next week. A good shepherd learns to look further ahead.

How does this book differ from my earlier ones, notably *Planning a Year's Pulpit Work* and *The Preparation of Sermons?* Chiefly in this respect, that I now deal in more detail with one kind of biblical preaching. This work differs also in the content of the cases, nearly all of which deal with Bible passages that I have not treated elsewhere in print. As a rule I aim to develop each case only far enough to make the idea clear, and then to suggest a trail for someone else to follow. By the use of cases from the Bible I wish to bring out the principles more or less inductively.

To pastors on the field, many of whom I have not met, I feel grateful for reports and questions about expository preaching for today. To seminary students, past and present, I owe much for what they have helped me learn about this elusive subject. To divinity schools where I have lectured on the subject I feel a sense of increasing obligation. To professors of English at Harvard years ago I am indebted for an introduction to the principles that undergird exposition, and for encouragement to use concrete cases. To the editors, to my chaplain son, to another son, and to my wife, as to librarians and colleagues past and present, I express appreciation for expert assistance. To Robert J. Robinson, graduate student, I am indebted for help with the proofs, and in many other ways. Most of all, to the Lord God I give thanks for the Holy Scriptures, and for the assurance that the Spirit will guide us mortals in using them to His glory.

ANDREW WATTERSON BLACKWOOD

CONTENTS

CONTENTS

CHAPTER ONE

THE WAYS OF EXPOSITORY PREACHERS

OPINIONS DIFFER WIDELY ABOUT THE MEANING AND the use of expository terms.[1] In the present book preaching means the interpretation of life today, in light that comes from God today, largely through the Bible. Expository preaching means that the light for any sermon comes mainly from a Bible passage longer than two or three consecutive verses. This kind of message differs from a textual sermon chiefly in the length of the Bible passage. In any case the wise interpreter begins with a human need today, and chooses a passage that will enable him to meet this need.

Whatever the description, expository preaching worthy of the name affords pleasing variety. The content and the form of such pulpit work ought to vary according to the human need in view, the Bible passage in hand, the personality of the man in the pulpit, and the spirit of the day in which he preaches. "Today is not yesterday." Instead of struggling to formulate a philosophy to account for these variations, let us look at certain expository preachers in the English-speaking world. We can do no better than to begin with Robertson of Brighton, who has become well known through his textual sermons,[2] and with Alexander Maclaren (or McLaren), who has won distinc-

[1] See Faris D. Whitesell, *The Art of Biblical Preaching* (Grand Rapids: Zondervan Publishing House, 1950); also Frederick B. Meyer, *Expository Preaching Plans and Methods* (New York: George H. Doran Co., 1912).

[2] See *Sermons Preached at Brighton*, four vols. in one (New York: Harper & Bros., n.d.).

tion as "the prince of expositors." By study of these men, as well as more recent expositors, we should see more clearly the meaning of such pulpit work.

1. FOLLOWING AFTER F. W. ROBERTSON

"We need preachers who could do for this generation what Robertson of Brighton did for his." So says Dr. W. R. Matthews, Dean of St. Paul's in London.[3] He refers to the fact that for six years, starting in 1847, at the age of thirty-one, Robertson engaged in a teaching ministry, based on the Bible. After his death, at the age of thirty-seven, he gradually became perhaps the most influential book preacher in the past one hundred years. Before he went to Brighton young Robertson had floundered, but there he soon established himself as a strong pulpit interpreter of the Bible. During those last six years he opened up the Scriptures twice on each Lord's Day, except in vacation time. In no case does he seem to have announced sermon topics in advance of delivery.

At the two services Robertson dealt with the Bible in two different ways. For want of more exact labels, his way of preaching in the morning has become known as textual, and in the afternoon as expository. More accurately, nearly all his pulpit work might bear the name of popular Bible exposition. At each service he dealt with truth and duty as he found them in a certain portion of the Bible. The basic distinction between his pulpit work in the morning and that in the afternoon appears in his own words:

We began two years ago the practice of giving the Sunday morning to a sermon, and the afternoon to a lecture. And the difference between the two was that in the morning we took for our subject some single text and endeavoured to exhaust it; but in the afternoon a chapter, and endeavoured to expound the general truths which

[3] See *Strangers and Pilgrims* (London: James Nisbet & Co., 1945), p. 6.

14

were contained therein. The sermon was hortatory and practical; the lecture was didactic. The first appealed rather to the heart and to the conscience; the second rather to the intellect and the analytic faculty.[4]

Evidently a "lecture" here means an expository sermon as part of a fairly consecutive course from a book of the Bible. During those inconspicuous years at Brighton the young interpreter took his Sunday afternoon hearers through the following books of the Bible, in this order: I and II Samuel, the Book of the Acts, Genesis, I and II Corinthians. The "lectures" from Genesis and from Corinthians found their way into print; those from Samuel and from the Acts did not. From various points of view the messages from Corinthians impress many of us more favorably than the earlier ones from Genesis. Even Robertson had gradually to master the art of dealing with a fairly long passage in a fairly short sermon. He must have "learned to do by doing." While lecturing week after week, except during holidays, he gained increasing mastery of an expository method. In Genesis he worked as a rule with the chapter as the source of the message. In Corinthians he tended to single out what we today call a literary unit. In these last and best examples of his published expository work Robertson tended to preach from shorter passages than in his earlier efforts.

In our present stress on Robertson as an expositor let us remember that he has gained posthumous distinction as a preacher of textual sermons. A textual sermon here means one where the basic structure corresponds with the main parts of the text. The difference between Robertson's textual sermons in the morning and his expository lectures in the afternoon appears in the printed accounts of what he did in the

[4] Written Feb. 17, 1850. See *Notes on Genesis* (London: Kegan Paul, Trench, & Co., 1886), p. 1.

pulpit on two successive Sundays in 1850. On the morning of August 4 Robertson spoke textually from Eph. 5:17-18, "Sensual and Spiritual Excitement." The next Sunday morning he dealt textually with Tit. 1:15, "Purity." With typical Robertsonian love of "two contrasting truths," the sermon began:

For the evils of this world there are two classes of remedies—one is the world's, the other is God's. . . . The world says, Give us a perfect set of *circumstances,* and then we shall have a set of perfect men. . . . Christianity . . . proves that the fault is not in outward circumstances but in ourselves.[5]

The body of the sermon dealt first with "The apostle's principle. . . . Each man creates his own world." Second, "The application of the principle. . . . It is not the situation which makes the man, but the man who makes the situation." "We do not want a new world, we want *new hearts.* . . . To the pure all things will be pure." A fitting message, for Brighton is a popular seaside resort, especially in midsummer.

On the afternoon of August 4 Robertson passed by Gen. 20, and spoke from chapter 21. According to the printed records, out of the fifty chapters in Genesis he dealt with only thirty. On the afternoon of August 11 he took up chapter 22, "The Temptation of Abraham." [6] As often elsewhere in his printed sermons, the interpreter made a problem approach. Even though he drew the supporting facts from the passage in hand, he must have made every hearer feel at once, "All of this concerns me today." In the body of the discourse Robertson showed the difficulty of what God asked Abraham to do in offering up his son, the inner meaning of this trial, and the way he met it triumphantly through faith.

Not only does this message show ability to interpret a passage

[5] See his *Sermons Preached at Brighton,* pp. 510-16, 516-21.
[6] See his *Notes on Genesis,* pp. 53-61.

from Genesis. Better still, the lecture reveals rare insight into the workings of the human heart. Best of all, the preacher shows how to touch the broken heart with a healing hand like that of the Divine Physician. Largely because of this ability to use the Written Word of God in meeting the heart needs of men and women, one by one, Robertson's afternoon expositions may have made a still more lasting impression, locally, than his more striking morning sermons. So if any reader wishes to study a master of expository preaching, he may well begin with the work of F. W. Robertson.[7]

2. LEARNING FROM ALEXANDER MACLAREN

The textual sermons and the expository messages of Alexander Maclaren (1826-1910) show a homiletical experience different from that of Robertson. If Maclaren had gone home to God at the age of thirty-seven, he might never have become known as "the prince of expositors." This part of his preaching experience began late rather than early. At the age of thirty-three he issued the first volume of sermons, mainly textual, and after that he sent out many other volumes, containing only an occasional exposition of a longer passage. As a rule, until after middle age, he gave the preference to textual preaching. For example, take the message from Isa. 12:3, "With joy shall ye draw water out of the wells of salvation" (K.J.V.) [8] His topic was "The Wells of Salvation." After an introduction about the historical setting, he spoke on the meaning of the wells, the ways of drawing water, and the joys of those who draw. By joys he meant the heart satisfactions of those who by faith found spiritual refreshing in the Bible, the Church, and other visible

---

[7] See James R. Blackwood, *The Soul of Frederick W. Robertson* (New York: Harper & Bros., 1947); also Stopford A. Brooke, *Life and Letters of Frederick W. Robertson*, 2 vols. (London, 1873-75).

[8] See *The Secret of Power* (New York: Macmillan & Co., 1882), pp. 212-21.

means of grace. In passing he called attention to a contrasting text: "Sir, thou hast nothing to draw with, and the well is deep" (John 4:11*a*, K.J.V.) . The sermon included almost nothing about Isa. 12:1-6 as an inspired poem.

Occasionally in his earlier books Maclaren showed increasing mastery of an expository method. In preaching about "The Shepherd King of Israel" the interpreter dealt with Ps. 23 as a whole. Instead of always feeding his sheep with a "three-pronged fork," as many of us were taught, Maclaren let the form of his passage determine the structure of his sermon.[9] In Ps. 23 he saw reason for only two main divisions, with subdivisions clearly marked. Differing as the two men did in many other ways, both Maclaren and Robertson excelled in crystal clarity, partly due to careful use of structure. Even more than the other man, Maclaren excelled as a student of the Bible, beginning with the original languages. Now let him interpret Ps. 23:[10]

Introd.—The experience of David as a shepherd
  I. The Divine Shepherd and His leading of His flock (vss. 1-4)
    A. God leads His sheep into rest.
    B. He also leads us into work.
    C. He leads us through sorrow.
  II. The Divine Host and the guests at His table (vss. 5-6)
    A. God supplies our wants in the midst of strife.
    B. He cares for our needs in this life.
    C. He brings us hope for the life to come.
Concl.—Take this psalm as your own, by faith.

After he had passed middle age, Maclaren began to do expository work regularly. In later years he seems to have

---

[9] In *The Secret of Power*, one of his ablest volumes, he had seven three-point sermons and fourteen four-point. This, however, was exceptional.
[10] See *Sermons Preached in Manchester*, first series (London: Macmillan & Co., 1882) , pp. 307-18.

devoted himself almost exclusively to exposition, both in the pulpit and as an author. In this later period he sent out a commentary on Colossians and Philemon and one on the Psalms, both in *The Expositor's Bible.* After his retirement in 1903 he began the preparation of his *Expositions,* which he selected from the public work of the past years. The two commentaries he prepared after he began to lecture, at a time when many ministers have crossed the dead line, intellectually. Unfortunately the date of the following incident does not appear in the biography, but the change over to regular expository work seems to have come in his fifty-seventh year, not long before his wife went home to God (1884).

It was often so difficult for Dr. McLaren to choose a text that at times he sighed for the old-fashioned Scottish habit of lecturing through one of the books of the Bible, but he thought an English audience would not stand it.

On one of these occasions his wife advised him to try the experiment, and suggested the Epistle to the Colossians. He took her advice, but she did not live to hear all the sermons, which formed the nucleus of the volume Colossians in the *Expositor's Bible.* In it many of those best competent to judge consider Dr. McLaren reaches his high-water mark as an expositor.[11]

Except to an experienced interpreter, such as Maclaren, past middle age, consecutive expository sermons from Colossians would have seemed like a colossal task, demanding powers close to genius. What a difficult epistle, and what a worthy commentary! Maclaren's next adventure in expository preaching led to the Psalms, a much easier field. This work he began to publish at the age of sixty-seven. From that time forward, during his seventeen years on earth, the "prince of expositors" might have sung with Robert Browning:

[11] See *Dr. McLaren of Manchester* by E. T. McLaren, his cousin and sister-in-law (London: Hodder & Stoughton, 1912), pp. 224-25.

Grow old along with me!
The best is yet to be,
The last of life, for which the first was made.

Living daily with the Book, and working daily with his pen, Maclaren kept from crossing the dead line before he died, at the age of eighty-four.

Any pastor who wishes to engage in research at home can study comparatively the textual sermons and the expository messages in the works of some other strong preacher of sermons now in published form. Think of William M. Taylor, with the contrast between his popular morning sermons in *Contrary Winds* or *The Limitations of Life,* over against the second-service messages in the book about the parables or the one about the miracles. Compare the volume of striking sermons by George Adam Smith, *Forgiveness of Sins,* with his brilliant treatment of the minor prophets. All of this about the prophets appears in *The Expositor's Bible.* Apply the same method to the published works of John Henry Jowett, G. Campbell Morgan, Alexander Whyte, Joseph Parker, R. S. Candlish, John Calvin, or any other master interpreter who has written freely for the press. For obvious reasons the list does not include any preachers now living. Many of them appear as editors and authors of the new commentary with a name suggested by John Bunyan's "house of the Interpreter." [12]

3. HEARING FROM RECENT EXPOSITORS

The men in view thus far belonged to yesterday, or the day before. Later ministers have witnessed a turning away from expository preaching, with a turning toward a larger use of topical sermons. A topical sermon here means one where the

[12] See *The Interpreter's Bible,* 12 vols., issued semiannually, beginning 1951, by Abingdon-Cokesbury Press, New York and Nashville.

content and the form of the message owe more to the topic than to the text or the passage. During the secularizing years that followed World War I, many pulpit masters in our land felt that it was no longer possible to do expository work. With a sort of nostalgia Joseph Fort Newton wrote after his return from a pastorate at the City Temple in London, "Expository preaching, so fruitful in other days, [is] well-nigh impossible, at least in America, where life moves to the rhythm of motors, movies, and jazz." [13] That statement must have been too sweeping. A few years after he penned that lament, Newton delivered an expository sermon from Isa. 6:1-8. Except near the end, where he made a summary, instead of appealing to the will of the hearer, the interpreter held us all spellbound. He showed how a young man of today needs a vision of the Holy God.

Friendly observers from abroad did not all agree with Newton and many other American divines about the impossibility of doing expository work here in the States. Once again the testimony must come from a man no longer in the flesh. The late James Black would not have cared for our labels, but he excelled at times both in textual and in expository preaching. As with most expositors in recent decades, he planned to begin either sort of sermon with a text and a topic. Not long before his decease he delivered at the Princeton Seminary summer Institute of Theology a semiexpository sermon from Luke 4:16-22, under the heading "He came to Nazareth."

Despite insufferable heat that sermon gripped and held every hearer. Without Black's personality, and his gifts of imaginative utterance, the message appears in his posthumous book of sermons, *Days of My Autumn*.[14] The volume includes a still abler sermon, biblical if not expository, "The Man That

---

[13] See his book *The New Preaching* (Nashville: Cokesbury Press, 1930), p. 116.

[14] London: Hodder & Stoughton, 1950. Pp. 44-54.

Made the Earth Tremble" (Isa. 14:16).[15] As Black delivered it, the discourse must have made shivers run up and down the spinal column of every hearer with red blood. Without naming a single modern dictator, the interpreter led everyone to see the folly of trembling before any "sparrow of a man." In the eyes of God, "only the good man is great." All of this shows James Black as no mere armchair critic of American preaching during its doldrums. What follows relates to yesterday.

What did this master think of our pulpit work here in the States two decades ago? Especially in summer he used often to preach in and about New York City, in communities where most of the pastors protested that they could not get a hearing for expository sermons. Black's experiences, often repeated, led him to the opposite conclusion. He found that laymen relished his kind of expository fare, even in midsummer. After an expository message from a number of consecutive verses in Philippians, the lay officers of a certain large church surrounded him and asked, eagerly:

"Why can we not get that type of preaching more often in America?" "This proves," wrote the Scotsman, "that your thoughtful church people are not so enamored of your topical preaching as many of your ministers suppose. . . . In the end this kind of preaching kills itself. . . . It ruins a man's message, his own spiritual balance, and his people's outlook. . . . As preachers we have Jesus Christ and His teaching and doctrine to proclaim. Everything else is secondary to that." [16]

4. ENCOURAGING THE YOUNG INTERPRETER

Today the tide seems to have turned, though there has been nothing in the form of a tidal wave. An increasing

[15] *Ibid.*, pp. 89-100. (All the book does not move on this level.)
[16] See "Some Honest Impressions of America" in the *Christian Herald*, Feb., 1933. Used by permission of the author.

number of ministers on our side agree with James Black about the possibility and the wisdom of doing popular expository work, though not exclusively. Many of them have begun to seek after ways and means of preparing this kind of sermon, with the stress on preaching rather than exposition. The recent experience of one young interpreter will show the adventurous spirit that should characterize the expository work of tomorrow. A few years ago, when about the age of young Robertson at Brighton, Dr. John S. McElroy became pastor of the large downtown Arch Street Methodist Church in Philadelphia. In one of my books the young minister found suggestions about using some of the psalms as the basis for popular sermons during midsummer. Wisely he determined not to begin preaching such messages of his own making until he had learned all that he wished to know about the best of books in the heart of the Bible. For eighteen months, while preaching from other parts of Holy Writ, he lived with the Psalms, and with books about the Psalms. At last he felt ready.

In June and July he delivered a series from the Psalms, both at the morning service and, more briefly, over the radio. Those messages brought the pastor and his hearers so much enduring satisfaction that he reports having kept on preaching from the Psalms more or less ever since. Naturally his way of dealing with them differs widely from that of Robertson or Maclaren, and from the suggestions that appear in the following chapters. The young pastor's courage in turning to the Psalms for use in a downtown church during the summer, and especially in taking up the most difficult of them all, the 139th, led me to ask for the statement that follows. May this statement encourage many another Bible interpreter, young in heart, if not in years, to start out on some such glad adventure of faith and hope.

23

The psalm was used with an interpretive scripture lesson, and the same psalm was selected as the responsive lesson. As much as possible I sought to use the words of the psalm as an expression to identify and describe experiences and emotions that come into every life today. The list of subjects follows, with a sentence or two [by Dr. McElroy] to describe the intent or direction of the sermon.

"How to Go to Church on Vacation" (Ps. 15). The psalm teaches us to change "how" to "who." What in us pleases God when we go to church?

"When Vows to God Are Valuable" (Ps. 116:18). God must deal with each of us in terms of promises to Him.

"When Pain Makes You Bitter" (Ps. 73:16-17). A "television screen" is available where one can sit down and see oneself in the eyes of God.

"Why Temptations Come Back" (Ps. 46). A parallel is drawn between times then and now. America needs a revival of religion to give faith instead of fear of an atomic war.

"The Surgeon of the Soul" (Ps. 139). Like a surgeon's knife that lays bare the secrets of the soul is the conviction that God knows, and guides.

"God's Prescription for Your Complaint" (Ps. 103). Spiritual talking to self recognizes God's many healings. Today's complaint of insecurity is answered by age-old faith.

"The Thank-Offering Psalm" (Ps. 100). The Christian meaning is shown of the claim of faith, "We are His." It is the faith of the Hebrew fathers and of the Pilgrims, a faith that marches while it sings.

Even though the tide in our day seems to have turned, not every reader may feel ready as yet to launch out on such an adventure of faith. Still less does every pastor feel able with Robertson or Maclaren to lecture through a major book of the Bible. Even so, let everyone remember the varieties of expository work. Why not begin now to prepare a single expository sermon? It may be from one of the simplest psalms. If anyone would know how to begin, he may turn to the following chapters. First let him ask the Spirit of God to shine upon the open page and bring the truth to light in the face of Jesus Christ. Then the venture of faith will be begun, continued, and completed in the spirit of prayer.

Some of our ablest interpreters from yesterday never did give up their belief in expository preaching. One of them, who differs from Maclaren in doctrine and in many other ways, seems equally unwilling to cross the dead line before he dies. At the age of seventy-five, Dr. Raymond Calkins wrote in *The Romance of the Ministry* concerning the parish minister looking back upon his life: "I would like to live it all over again. For my life has been pure poetry, real romance from first to last. There is no more romantic career than that of a minister of Jesus Christ." During the succeeding eight years Calkins has done more than one piece of major expository writing. Some of the reasons for his joy appear in the following excerpts from *The Romance:*

A true sermon always has humanity within it and divinity behind it.

Good sermons usually have a long history. They mature slowly. They are not made between Sundays. A week is too short a time for an idea to germinate, grow, blossom into full bloom. . . . The preacher will have scores of sermons . . . slowly maturing. His question is not what to preach, but only what to preach next. . . .

The preacher will be a continuous and profound student of the Bible. To the neglect of the Bible may be traced many of the shortcomings of the pulpit. Too much modern preaching has lost touch with the Bible. It does not talk in Bible language, it does not deal with Bible themes, it does not proclaim the Bible message. . . . Bible preaching never runs dry or grows thin. . . . There are never enough Sundays in the year for Bible truths that clamor for utterance.

Expository preaching is rich with possibilities both for the preacher and for the congregation which delights in it. By this is

25

not meant a long series of sermons from one Bible book, but occasional sermons expounding some portion of Scripture. . . .

All such preaching is interesting. It is also fructifying. It touches always on the permanent issues of life. And it gives the Bible back to the people.[17]

[17] From *The Romance of the Ministry* (Boston: Pilgrim Press, 1944), pp. 253, 155-58. Used by permission.

CHAPTER TWO

THE GOALS IN EXPOSITORY PREACHING

AS A PROFESSOR AND LATER AS HEAD OF THE SOUTHERN Baptist Theological Seminary at Louisville, John R. Sampey wisely felt that he ought to keep in touch with the life and work of a local church. So he served as pastor of a rural congregation not far from the city. At the age of fifty-seven he began doing regular expository work, which he continued to the end of his days. He began preaching from the Bible the way it was written, a book at a time, with sermon units longer than single verses.

In preaching from the Acts, or the Fourth Gospel, this teacher of the Old Testament would ask the people each time to read the next two chapters. His *Memoirs*[1] do not tell all the details, but they make clear his delight with the effects among the people, and his wonder that he had waited for years before he began to feed the flock this way. In a conference with ministers he once explained the general plan, and he led all of us to wonder why it had not become common. Whatever the procedure, the blessings among the people must come from God. He has a way of blessing the proper use of His Written Word.

Let us assume that a pastor sets out to learn how to prepare and deliver effective expository sermons, so that he may

---

[1] See the *The Memoirs of John R. Sampey* (Nashville: The Broadman Press, 1947) , pp. 166-67.

give some such message almost every week. What should he hope to accomplish among his people?

1. REDISCOVERING THE BIBLE

Intelligent preaching of this kind helps the people to rediscover the Bible. In a certain congregation of the Middle West the people kept reading the Third Gospel, and later the Acts. Each Lord's Day they followed the pastor as he opened up a portion of what they had been reading. They did not know in advance which paragraph he would single out, since he did not take up passages consecutively. In time they got to feel at home in each of those Bible books. Later a young businesswoman reported: "I have been coming to church and Sunday school all my life. Never until lately have I learned how to read and enjoy the Bible. I can shut my eyes and see two Bible books as clearly as I can see *Hamlet* and *Macbeth*. I am also learning how to look at a paragraph as a whole, and how to live on the Bible in my daily work downtown." Another young businesswoman declared: "I can see the Book of Acts as clearly as a cameo."

One morning the pastor spoke about "An Unexpected Answer to Prayer." Often he had preached on prayers unanswered. This time he stressed what the Bible teaches, that God always answers real prayers, but not always at once, and not always affirmatively. Instead of arguing about the matter, or theorizing, on the basis of his own imperfect experiences, the pastor dealt with a Bible case. In Acts 12:1-17 he found all the biblical materials he needed for a case study. In this passage he saw Christian men and women praying together, and at the same time refusing to believe that God would answer their prayers. The resulting sermon discussed the matter largely in present tenses.

I. A clear case of united prayer
   A. Prayers for a prisoner facing death
   B. Prayers for his deliverance
II. A clear case of answered prayer
   A. Release from prison and death
   B. Release through divine intervention
III. A clear case of incredulity
   A. The amazement of a maidservant
   B. The unbelief of people at prayer
The power depends on God, not on us.

In using this case the pastor dealt with a problem that faces every believer today. Little by little this kind of preaching led the people to a rediscovery of the Scriptures as a library of the Christian religion for today. In a southern city a prominent architect recently told a visiting minister: "I have been reading the Bible and attending church all my life. Never until the last few years have I looked on the Scriptures as a library full of cases about religion and life for today. We use the case method in the study of medicine and law, engineering and business administration, why not in teaching and preaching practical religion?" Under the leadership of the home pastor, in the pulpit and elsewhere, the architect and other members of the congregation have learned to use the Bible as a guidebook for everyday living.

Laymen everywhere wish to make this kind of rediscovery, but many of them do not know how. When they turn to books on the subject, they find meaty volumes that puzzle inexperienced seekers. In a certain large city a group of able young business and professional people of both sexes come together once a week to discuss "The Rediscovery of the Bible." Instead of going to the Bible itself, they follow an up-to-date guidebook in which a scholarly writer surveys everything broadly, and leaves the inexperienced lay reader with a lot of confused impressions concerning things biblical.

One evening the group took up the question "Why Must a Good Man Suffer?" though they phrased it in the plural. In the Book of Job the Bible deals with this problem, but not simply. Instead of trying to figure out the meaning of this one Bible book, or of some simpler Bible teaching on the subject, the young seekers followed the guidebook in discussing the problem as it appears in eight difficult books of the Bible. They surveyed eight books in less than an hour. No one present seemed to have read any of the Bible books, not even Job, which the leader of the discussion persisted in pronouncing Jŏb.

What do these able and eager young college and university graduates need? They need a plan that will encourage them to read the Bible itself, one book at a time, and to start swimming in a small pool instead of out in the Atlantic. They also need someone to guide them in making the most of the Bible book in hand. "Do you understand what you are reading?" said an old-time believer to a talented seeker after God, who was perplexed about a Bible passage. "How can I, unless some one guides me?" (Acts 8:30-31.) In the Greek the word "guide" here means to "exegete." This in turn means to "lead out," to "explain and illuminate." In our day, with all of its uncertainty and confusion about the content and the form of the Holy Scriptures, who better than the home pastor can guide lay readers of the Book? This does not refer to experienced saints, but to bewildered seekers. The situation does not call for dry-as-dust expositions, but for bright-as-light adventures into "the book nobody knows." Oh, for another Protestant Reformation, with a rediscovery of the Holy Scriptures as the Written Word of God for today! Any pastor can have this kind of Reformation and rediscovery in the local church.

2. GROWING IN CHRISTIAN KNOWLEDGE

Among churchgoers expository preaching worthy of the name also results in growth of Christian knowledge. Largely through no fault of their own, countless regular church attendants remain religiously illiterate. They do not know what to believe, doctrinally, or how to live, ethically. Many of them, theoretically, believe in the Bible as "the only infallible rule of faith and practice," but they look on it, actually, as a closed book, except for the minister, who knows it well enough to select juicy and spicy texts for inspirational talks. To these sweeping statements anyone can think of many wholesome exceptions.

On the other hand, booksellers report that countless laymen have been reading nonbiblical books about what to believe, and how to live. Better still, hosts of laymen have been purchasing the Bible, especially the Revised Standard Version. Now they are looking to the pastor to show them how to read it as God's Book for busy people today. They want to grow in Christian knowledge. Only at the peril of his soul dare any local leader ignore this present-day desire for a larger and more intelligent use of the Bible. If any pastor does not know how to employ it in preaching, he can learn.

Unfortunately, many of these lay seekers after Christian knowledge feel perplexed and bewildered by most of the books about the Bible. They do not know how to digest the sort of volumes that appeal to men with seminary training. Neither do many laymen know how to apply a man's biblical sermons if he talks in terms of Kierkegaard and Eichrodt.[2] Both in Europe and here at home mighty scholars have rediscovered the fascination and power of the Bible as the main

[2] See D. W. Eichrodt, *Theologie des Alten Testaments*, 3 vols. (Berlin, 1948), a work that merits translation into English.

source of theology. These men have sent out learned treatises that delight the hearts of ministers educated to appreciate biblical doctrine.[3] Among our laymen the tremendous thoughts of theological giants need to be "stepped down." This does not refer to any change of content, but only to simplicity of form. This in turn calls for the treatment of one segment of Christian truth at any one time.

Much the same principle holds true of electric power. From the Tennessee Valley mighty cables bring electric current to cities and towns far away. Fifteen years ago the cables passing over villages and farms carried power enough to lighten the load in thousands of villages and rural communities. Before that power could become available in any village or on any farm, the energy had to pass through a transformer. The current remained the same in quality, but the man in charge knew how to "step down" the power from above, so as to meet the needs of a dairy farmer. In this way more than 90 per cent of all farmsteads in the United States have been electrified.[4] Why should there not be a corresponding use of power and light, religiously, in every community today?

The local pastor ought to serve not as the source of spiritual power, but as the transmitter of what comes down from the hills of God. Power, power beyond the dreams of men. Light, light from the City of God. But "stepped down" so as to meet the everyday needs of men who cannot comprehend many of our pulpit abstractions about "Man" and the "Supernatural." The wise interpreter begins with his people where they are, religiously. Except for a blessed minority, who already know

[3] For example, see R. C. Dentan, *Preface to Old Testament Theology* (New Haven: Yale University Press, 1950); Rudolf Bultmann, *Theology of the New Testament* (New York: Chas. Scribner's Sons, 1951).

[4] See Marquis Childs, *The Farmer Takes a Hand* (New York: Doubleday & Co., 1952), p. 13.

how to use the Bible as a practical guidebook, he may safely assume that the people know little about such things. He should also take for granted that they have untold capacities for learning. Much as he might wish to preach "intellectual sermons," dealing with tremendous truths in scholarly fashion, he may have to adopt what Bushnell would term "a retail method" of revelation. A man like Milton would dare to

> ... assert Eternal Providence,
> And justify the ways of God to men.

But the wise pastor may content himself with singling out a Bible case that shows one aspect of this many-sided truth, the Providence of God.

Any sermon that deals with a specific case will leave many questions unanswered. If so, why not? "Rome was not built in a day." Neither does a congregation become biblically educated in a single Sunday. Arouse curiosity. Make people hungry for more. Get them to read the Bible at home, and to see in it cases about God's Providence, preferably in the life of a man like the friend in the pew. In congregations here and there all over the land pastors are leading their people to know the basic realities of the Christian faith. For instance, one minister recently faced a local situation that led him to deal with Acts 16:6-10.

When God Says No

God guides a man in unexpected ways.
He refused to sanction Paul's plan.
I. God's will for you may be yes or no.
   A. He wants to reveal His will.
   B. He expects one to follow.
II. His will may cause amazement and grief.
   A. He may close a door you wish to enter.

B. He may point to a path you do not like.
III. His way will seem best at the end.
   A. The Holy Spirit led Paul into Europe.
   B. He guides now into the best field.

In making ready for this kind of message review the masterly sermon by Horace Bushnell, "Every Man's Life a Plan of God." [5] Also use facts from the experiences of the Apostle, especially in this sixteenth chapter. Paul wanted to keep on at work in Asia Minor, but the Lord led him over into Europe. There he achieved his most amazing triumphs, and gradually he learned ways of wisdom in "handling life's second-bests."

The same truth often appears in biographies of other Christian heroes. Young Robertson set his heart on becoming a soldier, but God made him a minister. John L. Nevius wanted to labor in Alaska, but the Lord sent him to China. S. Hall Young longed to work in China, but the Lord gave him a commission for Alaska. Robert Morrison set his eyes on Africa, and God used him in China. In each case the man accepted the will of God, and soon began to find in it the highest earthly joys.

> Praise ye the Lord, who o'er all things so wondrously reigneth,
> Shelters thee under His wings, yea, so gently sustaineth!
> Hast thou not seen
> How thy desires e'er have been
> Granted in what He ordaineth? [6]

3. USING THE BIBLE PRACTICALLY

People who "sit under" the right sort of expository preaching form the habit of living all week according to what they

---

[5] See *Sermons for the New Life* (New York: Chas. Scribner's Sons, 1858), pp. 1-15.

[6] Hymn by Joachim Neander, "Praise Ye the Lord, the Almighty" (1680).

learn from the Bible. They begin to look on it as a contemporary book, grounded in history, full of light and power for today. In a certain capital city many young women and girl members of a downtown church made their living in offices and stores. Once every year the church set apart a Sunday evening in their honor. For them and their invited guests the minister preached a special sermon. From a different point of view each time he showed how some part of the Bible stood ready to help amid the trials and temptations of work downtown. One evening he dealt with the case in Acts 16:12-15, "The Religion of a Businesswoman." (From another point of view, "A Case Study in Adult Conversion." Use one subject or the other. Do not shift the camera.)

> I. This businesswoman attends church.
> II. She accepts Christ as her Saviour.
> III. She unites with the church by baptism.
> IV. She engages in Christian service.

This line of thought may seem obvious to us ministers. It did not prove so with those businesswomen and girls. Far from their homes out in the country, exposed to the loneliness and the allurements of a strange city, they felt the need of a religion that worked downtown in an office. In church they discovered that the Bible had to do with workaday tasks and needs. Better still, they found that God cared, and that He stood ready to meet the daily needs of every daughter. After that evening sermon about Lydia, a young businesswoman wrote as follows to the minister, whom she did not know, because she belonged to another church:

You have put new zest into me for the work in this office. As a girl in college I had set my heart on going out to Africa for lifetime mission service. When my dear father died suddenly, I had to come home and help support the family. I took a short business course, and then I began to work here. Up until now I have almost hated this place, and I have chafed under my daily load.

This morning I came in early and knelt down beside my desk to pray: "O Lord, let this place be for me today and every day the house of God and the gate of heaven. Help me here to serve Thee as gladly and well as I had hoped to serve Thee over in Africa."

Every pastor has had such heart-warming experiences. When he looks back, he discovers that many of them have come because of the Bible, rather than the preaching. After each fresh pulpit revelation of truth and duty the lay friend has a new incentive for home reading of the Scriptures and for prayer. From laymen who have rediscovered the Bible, and have begun to use it in daily living, the church school can recruit teachers. There they begin to understand the Book all the more fully because they keep using it to help others. Who can wonder that in a church with the right sort of expository preaching laymen keep growing in ability to live from the Bible? As Henry Drummond says, "Effects follow causes."

4. GROWING IN CHRISTIAN GRACE

"How can we get our people to grow in grace?" Grace here means the attractive goodness of God. The pastor and the lay officers keep asking how they can help to deepen the spiritual lives of the people in the home church. Here we consider one answer, though not the only one. Get them to think and live biblically. Gradually lead them to know and love such a Bible book as the Acts. For instance, take the matter of conversion. Instead of theorizing about it, or echoing the vagaries of certain high-pressure revivalists, take up case after case in the history of the Apostolic Church. No one in the sanctuary may have had any such experience as that of the Philippian jailer. Even so, everyone will gain much from a practical study of the way that man became a Christian. He appears to have been of middle age, and to have known nothing previously about the Bible (Acts 16:25-34).

A CASE OF CONVERSION IN MIDDLE LIFE

"You want me to become a Christian. Tell me how."
A Bible case shows facts about adult conversion.
I. It begins with a desire to become a Christian.
    A. The desire may come in various ways.
    B. It may lead to a talk with a believer.
II. It consists in receiving the Saviour.
    A. The convert knows and trusts Him.
    B. The convert gives himself into Christ's hands.
III. It issues in a life of service.
    A. This man first tries to undo a wrong.
    B. Then he unites with the church by baptism.

The sermon ought to stress what stands out everywhere in the Acts: Christian conversion leads to Christian service. First a beginning of the new life, and then growth through the exercise of redeemed powers. Technically speaking, regeneration leads to progressive sanctification, but why deal with a practical book of the Bible technically? Many cases in the Acts show that God uses practical means of transforming sinners into saints. Each time the details differ. In no case, however, ought we to think of evangelism and conversion apart from Christian nurture and growth.

All of this appears in the life and work of Dwight L. Moody.[7] At St. Louis he once preached about the conversion of the Philippian jailer. Knowing that the sermon would appear word for word in the morning newspaper, Moody planned to repeat his text nine times. "Believe on the Lord Jesus Christ,

[7] See Wm. R. Moody, *D. L. Moody* (New York: The Macmillan Co., 1930).

and thou shalt be saved, and thy house" (Acts 16:31, K.J.V.). In the city prison a notorious criminal named Valentine Burke saw the newspaper heading about a jailer being caught. Since he hated jailers, Burke read that sermon eagerly. Then he read it again. Through the aid of the chaplain, Burke became a Christian. During the rest of his life he showed the reality of his conversion by growing into the likeness of his Lord. In time he became the treasurer in the office of the sheriff, with direct responsibility for sums of money as large as $60,000.

After that conversion Moody became acquainted with Burke. Years later when the two met, the evangelist did not recognize the other man. With all his ability to remember names and faces, Moody felt sure that he had never seen the man before him. When Burke revealed his identity, Moody asked for two photographs, which he afterwards displayed in some of his meetings. One picture showed Burke the criminal; the other showed Burke the Christian. "If any one is in Christ, he is a new creation; the old has passed away, behold, the new has come" (II Cor. 5:17). Herein lies the secret of having people grow in grace. Let every one of them be "in Christ," and then trust Him to do the transforming.

This kind of transformation does not follow after much of our preaching from the Bible. As an extreme case, look at the sermon plan below. It deals with biblical ideas, and calls for biblical language. A man reasonably well informed could prepare to preach this way without opening his Bible or consulting any book about a Bible passage. Note how the hypothetical sky pilot dodges the heart of the matter, which is divine. In typically modern fashion, when a man has not taken time to prepare, this one discusses a positive subject negatively. While nobody ever perpetrated this particular piece of pulpit impertinence, I have heard much "preaching" of the sort by students who may have learned from us older men how not to preach from the Bible (Acts 16:30, 31).

What Must a Man Do to Be Saved?

Tell the story (5 min.), which the people have heard.
Luke tells it better, and briefly.
I. The importance of the question (10 min.). More important than any issue about a man's health, business, education, politics, the United Nations, *et al.*
II. The diversity of answers (10 min.). Down through the ages: Epicurean, Stoic, Aristotelian, Roman Catholic, *et al.*
The only answer that satisfies (1 min.).

"My, my," says the layman, "our pastor knows almost everything except how to answer a religious question biblically." If this layman went to a clinic to inquire about a spot on his face, what if a specialist spent half an hour talking about the case, discussing the history of cancer research, and dilating on the difficulty of curing certain varieties of this disease, and then sent the inquirer home? Much of our preaching, so called, consists in lecturing about sickness and health, with no attempt to remove the spot from the other man's soul. Yet we wonder why thoughtful men and women quit coming to church, or else attend where the physician of the soul excels in healing sin as the deadliest of all diseases.

5. APPLYING BIBLICAL ETHICS

The Lord blesses expository sermons also by using them to promote Christian ethics. Many of the major problems in our time have to do with morals. In public life we have witnessed a breakdown of ethical standards. In private living many of our people seem perplexed. Some of our young folk may feel tempted to indulge in premarital sexual relations.

So we might go on with diagnosis, most of it gloomy. Why waste time in elaborating what everyone knows? What can one do constructively? Why not begin to preach and teach the ethics of the Bible? Do not the Scriptures devote almost as much attention to duty as to doctrine? Of course the two belong together, but at one time a man stresses the doctrine that underlies a duty, and at another time the duty that grows out of a doctrine.

According to the ideals in the Acts, conversion normally leads to Christian ways of living, ethically. In a city of the South a leading churchman recently took up certain Bible cases dealing with controversial issues. Instead of attacking moral problems "head on," he approached each of them less directly. Among other issues he dealt with these: "Any Communism in the Early Church?" (Acts 2:43-47), "A Bible Case of Lynching" (Acts 7:54-60), and "When Segregation Seemed Sacred" (Acts 10). These messages received favorable attention from the daily press. Week after week the response among the hearers made the pastor feel that he should approach any moral problem biblically, and deal with any delicate issue indirectly.

In a city on the West Coast the Christian people became concerned about civic corruption, juvenile delinquency, and various other ills that thrive whenever Christianity languishes. By way of quickening the conscience of his people a pastor determined to follow the example of the prophets and the apostles in always "speaking to the condition" of the hearers. When Paul wrote to the "saints" at Corinth, he did not dodge any moral evil that plagued the city. In missionary labors elsewhere, also, his preaching led to moral reformation. For an example take Acts 19:11-20, "If God Had His Way in Our Community."

I. Believers would do mighty deeds (vs. 11).
II. Converts would burn some of their books (vs. 19).
III. God's cause would begin to prosper (vs. 20).

The "books" at Ephesus seem to have been scrolls containing the formulas, or "secrets," of magic arts that money lovers used in defrauding silly people. According to Moffatt's translation, those scrolls were worth two thousand pounds. In our denatured currency that might mean almost thirty thousand dollars. When those people in Ephesus became Christians, they saw the folly of using man-made ways of trying to get in touch with the Living God. In Africa recently a prosperous "medicine man" became a Christian. Then he destroyed all his paraphernalia for magic. As he told a friend, "Now that Jesus has spoken to me, the other voices do not speak."

Forty years ago the writer listened to an exposition of this passage. Throughout the years he has recalled the message, "When the Word of God Prevailed in Ephesus." He wondered then, as he wonders now, why the interpreter phrased his topic and discussed his subject almost wholly in terms of far away and long ago. In terms of today, rather than nineteen hundred years ago, what about the books and other printed matter that many boys and girls now read? As "literature," such publications differ from the scrolls in Ephesus, and perhaps the present ones do more harm. Somehow let us translate the Bible passage into thought forms of our time, and apply its teachings to the moral conditions of our homes. Ethical preaching from the Bible calls for courage and tact. Without courage and tact who can interpret the Bible for today?

6. DEEPENING CHRISTIAN EXPERIENCE

In this chapter the section headings overlap. So do the respective parts of the discussion. Nobody can divide the spiritual experiences of God's people into five or six segments. Now let us sum up the whole matter. Expository preaching tends to deepen the spiritual lives of church members. What else do the pastor and his wife long for so eagerly? Here again we should not oversimplify. God works in many ways to deepen and strengthen the spiritual experiences of His children. Among all these ways nothing stands out more often in church history than preaching from the Bible, in the spirit of prayer.

For an example of ways to deepen Christian experience turn to Acts 18:24–19:6, a passage about the need of the Holy Spirit. As with the church members at Ephesus, many of our people today have only a partial experience of God. They belong to the Lord, but they need to know Him better and love Him more. Such a state of affairs calls not for exhortation or scolding, but for teaching, in the spirit of love. When the gifted Apollos came to Ephesus, he fell in with Priscilla and Aquila, who taught him the way of God more perfectly. With the members of the church at Ephesus Paul did much the same. Then they received the Holy Spirit. Why? Largely because in Paul they had a "pastor" who taught them the same truths we now find in the New Testament. The power of the Holy Spirit came to church members through preaching and teaching, so that they learned to long for His presence.

The transforming power of expository preaching may not appear immediately. As a rule it takes time for good seed to result in a bountiful harvest. Over in New Jersey Benjamin Franklin used to plead with farmer friends to put lime on their land, so as to raise larger crops. When he found that they did not respond, he secured permission to try an experiment. Beside a public highway he chose a certain meadow. On it here and there he sprinkled plaster, which is powdered lime. After a while, because of sunshine and rain, everyone who passed that way could read in richer and fuller growth of grass the following inscription: "This Land Has Been Plastered."

A glance back over this chapter will show that under God almost everything in the local church depends chiefly on the pastor. If he becomes an expository preacher, worthy of the highest traditions, the congregation will benefit in ways beyond number. What of the effect upon the minister himself? To that important question we shall turn after we have considered practical ways and means of preparing expository sermons for today. So we shall think next about the choice of a suitable passage from the Bible.

CHAPTER THREE

THE SELECTION OF A BIBLE PASSAGE

UNDER GOD, THE EFFECTIVENESS OF AN EXPOSITORY SER-
mon may depend largely on skill and care in choosing
the passage. Instead of pausing to ask why, and to consider
the folly of certain selections, let us think about a few cases
from the Psalms. In the light of these cases the principles of
selecting a passage ought gradually to emerge. Why single out
the Psalms? Because many of these inspired songs lend themselves admirably to the uses of an expositor. If he thinks of
preaching in order to meet human needs, here and now,
where in the Bible can he find more in the way of truth and
duty for the needs of hearts today?

For example, make a working list of needs in the home
community, or in some larger sphere. Note that many needs
have to do with men and women one by one, others with the
home church or community, and still others with the nation
or the world. Then turn to the Psalms to see if you have on the
list any pressing need for which this Bible book does not
provide the making of a sermon. After one brief search, by
no means thorough, a student of the Bible and of preaching
came out with a list that he could have extended almost end-
lessly. In each case the verse gives the keynote, and the
message would come from the psalm as a whole.

A Psalm About the Nations (2:1)
A Bible Picture of Man (8:4)

A Guest in the House of God (15:1)
A Song About Forgiveness (32:1)
A Bible Cure for Despondency (42:11)
A Psalm for Days of Unrest (46:10a)
A Nation on Its Knees (85:4)
A Bible Secret of Security (90:1)
A Religion of Sheer Joy (103:1)

In preaching from well-known psalms a man has the advantage of beginning with inspired words that many of the hearers know and love. Churchgoers may not understand all of the Psalms, but the average hearer knows parts of this book better than any other portion of the Bible. He also loves the Psalms better. To these inspired songs he turns first when he wishes to find a word from God about any need of the heart. He would look to the Psalms far more often, and find in them far more of worth, if he had from the pulpit clear guidance about reading and understanding this part of Holy Writ. Why not let the interests of the hearer help to guide in the choice of the passage?

The inexperienced interpreter will find it relatively easy to prepare an expository message from one of the simpler psalms. Naturally, he should not begin with the 2nd, or the 139th, which would lead him into deep waters. Here and there he can find psalms so simple and moving that he should long to share them with lay friends in need of messages from God about things of deep concern today. How then should the inexperienced expositor go about choosing a passage from which he can draw a message for his friend in the pew?

1. ALLOWING ABUNDANCE OF TIME

A wise man allows abundance of time for any such project. He does begin by looking for preaching texts and sermon subjects. He may resolve first to master a certain book in the

Bible, such as the Psalms. With the aid of two or three standard commentaries, with another scholarly work or two about the Psalms, he may determine to study this Bible book itself, as a whole and in its parts. Hour after hour, day after day, while preaching from some other part of the Bible, he may live and move and have his being in this book, preferably starting with the original tongue. In case of difficulty he should turn to commentaries, but his main concern should be to know the Book of Psalms, both as a whole and in its most important parts.

A pastor at home can study the Psalms according to their purpose. Why not make a list of those that consist mainly of prayers, of praises, and of practical philosophy? The last term may seem loose, because of striving after alliteration. Any man who singles out the prayer psalms will find more of them than in either of the other groups. Also he will discover many praise psalms. As for the third group, whether in the form of testimony or of teaching, he will have at hand the making of a "Practical Philosophy According to the Bible." If to each psalm he gives a name showing its message for today, he will gradually begin to feel at home in this mountain country of the Bible.

Out of this Bible study may come, years from now, a series of messages about "The Psalter as a Book of Prayers," and later another series about "The Best of All Church Hymnals." Again, the pastor may have a series about "The Psalms as Guides for Living Today." Before he attempts anything so large and so difficult as a series, he should learn how to prepare and preach a sermon about a simple psalm all by itself. Thus the lay hearer can gradually become accustomed to this kind of biblical fare. If a minister does not become a master of expository preaching in one week, neither does a congregation acquire expository hunger all at once. As a rule, with numerous exceptions, both pastor and people must learn how to appreciate and enjoy this kind of sermonic food.

The preliminary study of the Psalms may continue for months, or even more than a year. If so, why worry? Keep on until you know this book more intimately and more lovingly than any other portion of the Bible. You will find that a hearer tends to remember a Bible message about as long after delivery as the interpreter has been thinking about it beforehand. For instance, take the first psalm, one of the simplest among all these inspired songs. Since it serves as the preface to the entire book, why not use these simple words in the first of many psalm-sermons that will continue at times through years to come? The following account may anticipate principles that will later stand out more boldly. If so, emphasis will come through intentional repetition.

In a rural parish one may use the subject "The Psalm of a Farmer." In a city church, "What the Bible Means by a Good Man." In either case the sermon may begin with the statement of a problem, perhaps indirectly. In the eyes of God, what does our country most need today? And our world? Character! In view of the moral breakdown on every side, what do we need so much as manhood? What sort of manhood and character? For a Bible answer we turn to the passage, with its two contrasting pictures. Note that the first psalm, like many another, is a "gift of God to the imagination."

I. The fruitfulness of God's tree. Perhaps the most beautiful things He has made
   A. Rooted near water—right with God
   B. Fruitful in season—a blessing to men
   C. Beautiful in itself—a life that pleases
II. The worthlessness of the world's chaff. Note that the Bible usually puts the good thing first.
   A. No roots—not right with God

No stability—no depth—no permanence
 B. No fruits—no asset to the community
 C. No beauty—nothing for a boy to emulate
Concl.—This depends on the aim of the preacher.

"Is that what you mean by an expository sermon?" Yes, in one of its myriad forms. Everything except the illustrative matter, chiefly from biography, may come out of the psalm. The sermon will help the hearer to interpret life today, in light from the first psalm. "What about the remainder of the song? What of the opening verse, with its three stages of climactic parallelism—walking, standing, sitting?" This has to do with a good man's friendships. "How can anyone deal with the first psalm without a study of the opening verse?" Herein lies one of the main facts about popular expository preaching. A man goes into the pulpit to meet a need, not to explain a passage. He wishes to preach a sermon, not to deliver a classroom lecture. In order to make a truth clear and luminous he may have to select and heighten certain parts of the psalm, while he may not mention other portions.

"The art of exposition consists largely in willingness to omit." So the experts at Harvard told us in our advanced study of English literature. On the other hand, many Bible expositors make sermons seem heavy by trying to include all that they know about each passage. Why not put away in the storeroom some of those notes about the first verse, and then use them later in a textual sermon with the topic, "What the Bible Says About a Man's Friends"? As for the message from the psalm as a whole, who but a genius could do more than make clear and memorable the two contrasting pictures of the tree and the chaff? Let the tree stand out in beauty against the western sky, and make the chaff seem dim and hazy, because it has "gone with the wind." Show the contrast between the two pictures. So simple, and in a way, so sublime! As the Supreme Lover of beauty, God alone can make a tree. We men make the chaff.[1]

2. APPEALING TO THE IMAGINATION

The resulting sermon will appeal to the imagination. This term here means God-given ability to see what lies hidden from other eyes, and then to speak so that the listener will become a seer. In the work of the expositor imagination ought to control at every stage. Doctrinally, one would speak in terms of guidance by the Holy Spirit. The poet who wrote the 1st psalm, or the 121st, enables many of us to behold truth and beauty that we might never have seen on land or sea. If the man in the pulpit enters into the spirit of the inspired psalm, he too can body forth "the forms of things unknown," and give

> ... to airy nothing
> A local habitation and a name.

Then the friend in the pew, if he has a "seeing eye," and a childlike heart, will catch "the vision splendid." He can take it home, share it with his loved ones, and live in its light until traveling days on earth are done.

A minister without imagination at work all the time should not attempt to deal with a psalm, or any part of Holy Writ, except certain prosaic passages not intended for use in public worship. As an example of a song shot through with imagination take "The Traveler's Psalm," the favorite of many railroad men, and of countless others who journey by land, sea, or air. The 121st psalm consists of four word pictures, each with a form of beauty distinctly its own. Elsewhere I have pointed

---

[1] See Chas. H. Spurgeon, *Spurgeon's Sermons*, 20 vols. (Grand Rapids: Zondervan Pub. House, 1952), VII, 293-310, "The Chaff Driven Away." (Reprint)

out the four parts of "A Psalm for Vacation Time." It tells about the God of the Waiting Hills, the Sleepless Watch, the Friendly Shade, and the Winding Road. This road leads at last to the City of God.

The traveler's psalm consists of Bible doctrine set to music. Everything here has to do with the Providence of God in the life of a man like one in the pew, with a million others. Six times the brief song rings out the word "keep," which is sometimes rendered by a kindred term, "preserve." "The Lord will keep you." At morning or at evening prayers, when one of us has returned from a journey, or is about to fare forth, we say in concert this pilgrim psalm. Then we kneel down to thank God for traveling mercies, or else we commit to the Father's care the one about to leave the family circle. At times our eyes fill with unshed tears as we remember a loved one who has heard the sound of the trumpet from the other side of the river. As Protestants we believe in the communion of saints, on both sides of the river that men call death.

> Though sundered far, by faith [we] meet
> Around one common mercy seat.

From the traveler's point of view think of a lonely pilgrim as he looks up to the mountains and beholds the tender mercies of his God. For what does the man of faith keep looking up? Why does he turn away from self and the things of earth? He looks up for help. The form of what follows owes much to a sermon by a favorite book preacher of today.[2]

LOOKING UP TO GOD'S HILLS

I. Looking up for help (vss. 1, 2)
II. Looking up for happiness (vss. 3, 4)

[2] See James S. Stewart, *The Gates of New Life* (New York: Chas. Scribner's Sons, 1940), pp. 21-31, "Why Be a Christian?"

    III. Looking up for health (vss. 5, 6)
        No need to worry about self, or others
    IV. Looking up for hope (vss. 7, 8)

"What right has anyone to see in the 121st psalm even a glimpse of the life everlasting? Do not many Bible scholars assure us that the Psalms say almost nothing about the life beyond?" Many of us do not agree with such sweeping statements about the Psalms. Even if we did so agree, we feel that a Christian minister should enter the pulpit to meet a need today, not merely to explain a psalm of old. Not as a historian but as Christ's interpreter he should look on this part of God's Written Word in radiance that streams from the face of Him "who abolished death and brought life and immortality to light through the gospel" (II Tim. 1:10b). Not only does the Living God promise to keep the pilgrim of faith as he journeys from home day by day, and year after year. The One who never slumbers or sleeps will also watch over the pilgrim when he goes out from earth to the unseen City of God.

If any young reader does not yet behold all of this in the passage, an elderly friend may pray for him, "O Lord, I pray thee, open his eyes that he may see" (II Kings 6:17b). On the other hand, one might use the psalm merely as a means of bringing out ingenious ideas of one's own. One might voice ideas that it does not suggest, ideas foreign to its spirit. For example, one of our ablest pulpit masters has a sermon, "Molehills and Mountains," all "based" upon this passage. The psalm says nothing about molehills, but the preacher devotes the first fourteen paragraphs to us and our molehills, leaving only three paragraphs for the God whom the man of faith beholds among the mountains. If imagination means God-given ability to see what a passage means, and then to help the lay friend see, what shall we term the homiletical habit of

51

seeing in a psalm what the poet never dreamed of putting there, and what no New Testament writer encourages us to believe? We all tend to preach this way, substituting man-made molehills for God-made mountains.

Why not test this matter of what to see in a psalm? In the home lead the children in repeating together and committing to memory one after another of these beautiful poems. Then watch how the boy or girl of eight or ten loves to give each psalm a name. In one family circle the father conducts brief devotions after the morning and the evening meal. Sometimes, for sake of variety, he asks, "Which psalm shall we say this time?" One child calls for "the tree psalm," another for "the shepherd psalm," and a third for "the hill psalm." In church one day during a sermon about "the tree psalm" a nine-year-old girl drew a picture of a tree. In like fashion the late William Lyon Phelps, of Yale, as a boy learned to love the Bible. He drew what he saw, whether in a psalm or in a parable. Then he looked again that he might draw all the better. In time he became a popular lay preacher. So does every true expositor use imagination. Not to do so with a psalm would mean to misrepresent this part of God's Written Word.

3. MEETING THE NEEDS OF PEOPLE TODAY

Thus far I have been assuming what I shall now stress. Give the preference to a passage that meets a present need among the people here in the home community. With an experienced expositor the need may relate to world brotherhood, world peace, world relations, or something else equally broad and high. For a while, however, rest content with a need and a passage less difficult and exacting. At any cost of pride and vainglory, resist the tendency to deal with a subject that may dazzle the hearers, without touching any heart need or helping to solve any life problem. Fortunately, ever since World War II old-fashioned pulpit pyrotechnics have become uncommon. Every man called of God to preach has become "hearer-conscious." Why not also become "psalm-conscious"?

For an example of a need, widespread and deep-seated, take the matter of church attendance as an expression of loyalty to Christ and the home church. In one of the large congregations of the South 2,200 members one year gave through the church treasury $158,000. Of this amount 685 members contributed $144,000, while the rest gave only $14,000. The generous donors practiced tithing; the others did not. Without knowing any more about the facts, one hazards the guess that these 685 members attended church regularly, and that the others did not. Herein lies the most pressing problem in the typical Protestant church of today—the lack of regular attendance by its own members.

Instead of exhorting or scolding, deal with the matter from the pulpit, and elsewhere, by teaching. Take the 122nd psalm. Look on it as "a song of ascents," which the boy Jesus must have sung with other pilgrims on the way up to Jerusalem to attend one of the feasts. In the psalm look on Jerusalem as a symbol of the local church. Then let the imagination work on the subject, "A Man's Loyalty to the Home Church." With Josiah Royce in *The Philosophy of Loyalty,* think of loyalty as the greatest thing in religion and life. Loyalty means "the willing, practical, thorough-going devotion of a person to a cause, as that cause is embodied in a person." More simply, loyalty means love in action. Christian loyalty means love for Christ and His Church.

How does a man show love to Christ by loyalty to the home church? Since the psalm falls into three parts, do not hold back from the old-time way of planning a three-point sermon. Expositbecause preaching itself is old-fashioned. So is church loyalty, and the Christian love from which it springs. Begin also to form the habit of expressing the main ideas in the form of simple sentences. Let every leading sentence embody the dominant idea of the main topic. In short, put up these old-fashioned truths in a few neat bundles that the hearer can take home and use there in understanding the psalm.

I. A man shows loyalty by his presence (vss. 1-2).
    A. The love of desire, when absent
    B. The love of delight, when present
    C. The love of devotion, always and everywhere
II. A man shows loyalty more by his praises (vss. 3-5).
    Think of a husband and father at home (Prov. 31: 28-31).
    A. Praising the church for its beauty
    B. Praising its appeal
    C. Praising its influence
III. A man shows loyalty most by his prayers (vss. 6-9).
    A. Prayers for peace—"the peace of God"
    B. Prayers for prosperity—soul prosperity
    C. Prayers for the pastor (Not in the psalm, but needed)

Of the three passages at which we have looked for preaching leads, this last may prove the most difficult. The resulting message may not seem inspiring or memorable. Why not? Partly because the song itself does not quickly and easily stir the imagination. But if a man begins to brood over this inspired poem, and keeps on doing so, in due time he will see it come alive. He will begin to behold in it truth and duty in living characters. Not every psalm, or every sermon, can hope to soar. On the other hand, the resulting sermon, like the psalm, ought to show the spirit of "marching upward to Zion," beholding the beauty of God's house, and pouring out one's heart for the church, the kind of church that the Saviour loved, and for which He died.

The three psalms are alike in the sense that each has to do with one person, in the presence of his God. This fact makes for ease of understanding and preaching. Whenever a Bible passage concerns one of God's children, and only one at a time, the interpreter should make this truth stand out. On the contrary, when the passage deals with a group or a throng—it may be with the nation or with the world—this also ought to become clear. Meanwhile many of us yield to the modern tendency of pluralizing and generalizing almost everything. Also we discuss a positive truth negatively—the easier way. Hence our pulpit work lacks the sort of variety that marks the inspired sources. The first psalm sings about a tree, one tree. The second speaks about the nations, all in the eyes of God. The ninetieth tells about "Our God, our help in ages past." The ninety-first glories in the goodness of God to one of His children. Why not form the habit of bringing out what the Lord caused to be written in each golden psalm? Whatever others may do, the expositor strives to make clear what the Book says, and nothing else, except as the Spirit guides him in showing what the truth means in the life of today and tomorrow.

4. SEEKING THE GUIDANCE OF THE SPIRIT

In this whole matter of choosing a Bible passage, the Spirit stands ready to guide. The Spirit does so, as a rule, in ways far from conspicuous and spectacular. He wishes the interpreter to employ all his God-given powers. On the other hand, when a minister works in the study, week after week, he finds that the ability to select the very best passage and then treat it in the very best way grows with use. If, like Maclaren during the major part of his long ministry, a man spends many of his waking hours trying to decide exactly which passage to preach, he need not worry. No child of God ever wastes an hour that he devotes to thinking and praying over the open Bible. Be sure, then, to start work in abundance of time. Sooner or later the "illuminating flash" will come. Then you can see how to select the right passage to meet the needs of lay hearers whom you love.

CHAPTER FOUR

THE GATHERING OF SERMON MATERIALS

T HE BEST SERMONS IN OUR DAY CONSIST LARGELY OF facts, all sorts of facts. They are not facts by themselves, like variegated shells lying on the seashore, but facts selected with care and used in preparing a message to accomplish the end in view. Ever since William James sent out his *Principles of Psychology* (1890) many of our ablest writers and speakers have gone back to the old Bible way of using facts to show the meaning of a religious truth, or the working of a moral principle. In a fashion all His own, the Lord Jesus taught and preached by the use of facts. Today by His Spirit He is waiting to guide in this sort of preaching from the Written Word.

The parables, for instance, "speak only of the things you can touch and see." Today many facts may serve as parts of a sermon fabric, that is, as bricks in the wall. Other facts may come later in the planning to serve as windows here and there. Homiletical literature abounds in counsels about ways and means of finding and using illustrations. Few writers have called attention to the wisdom of using facts in the main fabric of a sermon. Sometimes the student of preaching finds it hard to tell whether a certain fact or set of facts ought to serve as part of a main wall, or only as a window. For present purposes we need not think further about these homiletical distinctions. Whether we look on a certain fact as a building block or as a window, we should recognize this truth: In order to be popular and effective today an expository sermon ought to consist largely of facts, facts, facts. Where can one find them, with pleasing variety and ready for use?

1. TAKING MATERIALS FROM THE PASSAGE

Turn to the basic passage for nearly all of the biblical materials. In choosing a passage as the basis for an expository sermon, a man does well to look for a portion full of fact words. As a mature interpreter Maclaren could cope superbly with Colossians, but he could not have done so in his early years as a preacher from the Bible. Young Robertson showed wisdom in dealing with Genesis and Samuel, the Acts and Corinthians—each book full of facts interesting and pertinent today. If the man of Brighton had lived to mature years, he would doubtless have gone on to expound Bible books more difficult. Even so, he would have dealt with each truth or duty more or less factually. In any one sermon he would have taken the Bible facts mainly from his passage.

Herein lies one of the main principles in expository preaching. Both in the study and in the pulpit focus attention on your passage, and look at it in the setting where it appears. Such a passage as Ps. 27 contains more facts than anyone could use in a single message. Why then look for facts elsewhere in the Bible? Certain hearers may praise the minister who on each Lord's Day conducts a "Cook's Tour" through the Holy Scriptures. "Our pastor surely knows his Bible!" No doubt he does, but how long will he have to preach this way before his people begin to know the Written Word of God as it came into being, book by book, and unit by unit?

For convenience we shall look at only the first six verses of Ps. 27, "The Faith That Conquers Fear." Since the body of the sermon will come from the passage, the introduction may have to do with fear today. In this case fear relates to a soldier, whom we may picture as young. Here then emerges the aim of the discourse: to lead the young hearer today into a faith that will enable him to conquer every fear. When the late George W. Truett was planning to preach for a week at a university, he wrote to ask the student council what they wished him to do. In reply the young people sent a telegram with only one request: "Tell us what to do with our fears." In one of the resulting sermons he might have preached from this psalm, which tells how by faith a soldier conquers his fears.

I. The faith that wards off fear (vss. 1-3). Testimony
   from experience—not boasting, but exulting in God
   A. Faith that trusts God here and now (vs. 1)
   B. Faith that trusts Him because of yesterday (vs. 2)
   C. Faith that trusts Him for tomorrow (vs. 3)
II. The faith that triumphs over fear (vss. 4-6). Prayer for
   faith to conquer means more than warding off.
   A. Prayer for faith to dwell with God (vs. 4)
   B. Prayer for faith to find security in God (vs. 5)
   C. Prayer for faith to offer sacrifices to God (vs. 6)

This working plan may look wooden, and the sermon itself may sound prosaic, if not unreal. So does the drawing for the trellis of a grapevine, or the blueprint for a Dutch Colonial cottage, fail to stir the imagination. But the vine itself, or the cottage, would scarcely become a thing of beauty if there were no basic plan. With a self-made design at hand, the man in the study knows what sort of facts he will need to carry out his plan. Most of the facts he may state in thought forms of today, but first he must know them as they appear in the passage.

In terms of weaving cloth for a garment, the warp comes from the Bible passage. In thought forms of our time a man makes clear what the first three verses of the psalm tell about the way to ward off fear, and what the next three verses tell about the way to conquer fear, so that it will become a willing servant rather than a ruthless master. In short, explain and discuss.

Where necessary, repeat. If the truth still seems strange, or unwelcome, say it again and again, each time in a different fashion, but always persuasively. Little by little you can make Ps. 27 sound like the voice of Christian experience today. Here and there, both the explanation and the discussion, however winsome and appealing, may call for illustration.

2. RELYING MUCH ON ILLUSTRATIONS

The nature of expository preaching calls for skill and care in the use of illustrations. The heart of a man in the study ought to leap up when he recalls a case where the passage in view helped a person of the sort in mind. During World War I a young Southern kinsman of President Woodrow Wilson served as a driver in the Motor Ambulance Corps. Over in France one night with no lights on the car he and his buddy drove up toward the front line trenches. All at once, with shot and shell falling on every side, the lad from the South began to fear that he might grow afraid. Then he recalled the anthem that he had helped to sing as a member of the Chapel Choir at Princeton University: "The Lord is my light and my salvation; whom shall I fear? the Lord is the strength of my life; of whom shall I be afraid?" (K.J.V.) As soon as these words full of faith and hope began to sing again in his soul, the young man forgot all about his fears. That night he did his duty, and the next morning he was decorated for bravery.

In using all sorts of facts from life a man should be careful to state them correctly. Once in the South I preached from Ps. 27 and related the incident above. At the close of the service a gentlewoman came forward to say, "I am that boy's mother." A little later the friend at the organ told me, "I composed that anthem, and I was in charge of the Chapel Choir when that lad was at Princeton." To each informant I addressed the ques-

tion, not without forebodings, "Did I get my facts straight?"
Evidently I did, though I knew that in this one illustration I
might have made a score of mistakes, or even more. Think of
facts about the lad, the ambulance, the anthem, and the university. Even if the illustration met these tests, did it stand another one, still more searching? Did it, like the psalm, throw
the stress on faith in God and not on the fears of the soldier?

The latter half of the message calls for unusual care. At first
there may seem to be only a slight connection between warding off fears that still have power (vss. 1-3) and conquering
them by faith so that they become subjects (vss. 4-6). The
second part of the psalm calls for careful study. The resulting
sermon ought to make a certain truth clear and luminous: the
young man who comes to know God at home and in church
can find in Him the power to conquer every fear on the field
of battle. Even after the most skillful explanation, and the most
persuasive discussion, this lofty truth may call for a living example.

The present illustration comes from World War II. For a
year our chaplain son was stationed on one of the Solomon
Islands which was repeatedly bombed from the air by Japanese
pilots who knew how to strike terror into the hearts of the
stoutest Marines. In looking forward to the Christmas season
the chaplain wrote a letter to the home church, which had
granted him a leave of absence when he had offered to resign.
He said in part:

In hundreds of conversations, in foxholes and dugouts, in black-
out rooms and sick bays, in Higgins boats and in jeeps, I have come
to a strange conclusion. Men with Christian faith are able to hope,
and men without faith are not. Hope in the hearts of men with faith
is tied up with the events of the first Christmas Day, when the Almighty entered into a human body and soul to redeem the world
from sin. He did not come to make life easy, but to make men strong,

in a world where the Son of God could be crucified. The stubborn and unbending hope of the human heart is expressed in the words of our greatest hymn:

> Let goods and kindred go,
> This mortal life also;
> The body they may kill:
> God's truth abideth still,
> His kingdom is forever.

It takes a lot of dive bombers to worry a man who believes that.

3. USING FACTS ABOUT BIBLE CHARACTERS

Often the best illustration, or living object lesson, comes from another part of the Bible. In preparing to preach from Pss. 42 and 43, one should make a special study of the refrain: "Why are you cast down, O my soul, and why are you disquieted within me? Hope in God; for I shall again praise him, my help and my God." The title may be "God's Cure for a Man's Despondency." For an object lesson turn to a passage (I Kings 19) about Elijah's despondency after his sweeping victory on Mount Carmel (I Kings 18). The warp of the sermon may come from Pss. 42 and 43; the woof may consist of these facts about Elijah's despondency. That mightiest of God's spokesmen became as weak as water when he sat "down in the dumps" and wished that he might die. Not only do these facts about Elijah show the causes of a strong man's despondency, as well as the curse. They also bring to light the cure, which has to do with God. "Hope in God."

The same principle applies to Ps. 51, which many of us associate with King David. Whether or not these lines come from that king, they accord with his experience after dreadful debauchery when about fifty years of age (II Sam. 11–12). In the sermon from Ps. 51, the stress ought to fall, not on the sins of the king, and on the enormity of his transgressions, but on the mercy of his God. If there were time, one might preach an introductory sermon from II Sam. 12, where the forgiveness came through what we may call preaching, which really took the form of pastoral counseling. Then a message from Ps. 51 would deal with forgiveness through prayer. A third sermon, from Ps. 32, would show the praises that follow forgiveness. No man ever preaches too often about the forgiveness of sins, provided he deals with the subject personally and factually, as he finds this truth in Ps. 51, "drawn out in living characters."

Few of us ever can address kings. So let us think of David as "A Mighty Man on His Knees." Less personally, and with less appeal to imagination, the title may be "A Prayer for the Pardon of Sins." Once again, the warp of the message may come from the psalm itself. Beginning with the Hebrew, and enlisting the aid of commentaries, one ought to study in Ps. 51 the meaning of the various terms for sin, and of those that show forgiveness. In the sermon, if a man tried to deal with all of these facts, he could not lift the hearer up into the realm of greater visibility so as to behold the goodness of God today.

If only for the sake of keeping the sermon from seeming heavy, omit some of these details, and thus have time to interweave facts from the experience of David when he sinned. Before you do so, be sure to enlist the attention of the hearer. Is it possible for a man past middle age to find pardon, cleansing, and peace after he has committed the most dastardly sins that a man ever perpetrates? Then bring out the answer as it appears in the poetry of the psalm. Remember that according to Hebrew ways of worship and living there was nothing for David to do but cast himself on the mercy of God. Nowhere among all sacrificial rites of the Old Testament could the king find an offering for one who had been guilty of adultery, murder, and practical treason. Now behold this mighty sinner, past middle age, casting himself on what the fathers called the "uncovenanted mercies of God."

A MIGHTY MAN ON HIS KNEES

A statement of the problem, in terms of today
A case from the Bible, the best of casebooks
I. He begins with need of forgiveness (vss. 1-6).
    A. Casts himself on the mercy of God (vs. 1)
    B. Longs for the cleansing of his soul (vs. 2)
    C. Confesses his sins against God (vss. 3-4)
    D. Deplores his guilt before God (vss. 5-6)
II. He looks to God for cleansing (vss. 7-12). This develops
    the idea in vs. 2.
    A. Prays for purity like the snow (vs. 7)
    B. Asks for health in his soul (vs. 8)
    C. Longs for blotting out of his sins (vs. 9)
    D. Seeks the joys of a ransomed soul (vss. 9-12)
III. He promises to engage in service (vss. 13-17).
    A. Engages to win others for God (vs. 13)
    B. Vows to continue the worship of God (vss. 14-15)
    C. Casts himself on the mercies of God (vss. 16-17)
    "I am sure that of all the Psalms this is the most
    applicable to me."—Thomas Chalmers

All these ideas except the one from Scotland come from the psalm itself. Still they do not include the last two verses of the psalm, verses that a man should feel free to pass by. Even so, the plan as it appears above contains more ideas and word pictures than one could present in a popular sermon. One might try to do so at a Bible conference, or at a midweek service, but even there one would more wisely select and omit. The easiest way would be to have three sermons. The first would show the basic truth about a prayer for the pardon of sin (vss. 1-6). The second would take up the neglected truth that a polluted soul needs cleansing (vss. 7-12). The third would bring out a truth that few of us associate with the fifty-first psalm, or with the Old Testament (vss. 13-17). As in the churches of India, and elsewhere on mission fields, a man shows the reality of his repentance by the ardor of his service. This kind of Christian service calls for personal work, public worship, and private commitment. The spirit of the penitent appears in the noblest of evangelistic hymns:

Just as I am! Thou wilt receive,
Wilt welcome, pardon, cleanse, relieve;
Because Thy promise I believe,
O Lamb of God, I come!

4. DRAWING FROM MODERN BIOGRAPHY

In dealing with Ps. 51 the man who omits parts will have time to use an example or two from modern biography. The same holds true of Ps. 91, which contains more ideas than anyone could present in a single discourse with sufficient use of modern examples. In the latter psalm a singer voices a practical philosophy of life. He witnesses to a faith that enables a man to live without worry or hurry or flurry, and that in a world full of dread alarms. When the man in the pulpit interprets the spirit of this inspired song, full of confidence and hope, the friend in the pew may ask himself, "Does all of that still hold true? Does it apply to me, here and now?" Instead of stopping to argue about the matter, or else to prove it by logic, the interpreter can point to facts from biography. At a time when fiction has been receding from favor, because of its low quality, first-class biographies abound.

Take the life of John Buchan, or Lord Tweedsmuir, in *Pilgrim's Way*.[1] A reading of this autobiography, and of adventure tales like Buchan's *Mountain Meadow*, will bring the interpreter a new understanding of life, and a new insight into

[1] Boston: Houghton Mifflin Co., 1940, pp. 26, 167, 176.

the meaning of security. What this statesman writes about his early study of the classics holds true in reading books by John Buchan. They give "a standard of values. To live for a time close to great minds is the best kind of education. . . . They correct a man's passion for rhetoric. . . . No experience can be too strange and no experience too formidable if a man can link it up with what he knows and loves."

As a brilliant student of military matters, Buchan once appraised Lord Douglas Haig. Compelled to face all sorts of difficulties—with allies, colleagues, and the home government—that sturdy Scots commander in World War I regained his hold on the religion of his childhood. He entered into the work at hand with a covenanting zeal, "a constant sense of the divine foreordaining of life. . . . He found deep wells from which to draw comfort." What a sentence, especially when one remembers that the general discovered those deep wells in the Bible, not least in the Psalms. "He found deep wells from which to draw comfort." For example, look at Ps. 91.

The Bible Secret of Security

Introd.—The sentence from Lord Haig—for an example look at a case from the Psalms.
I. The meaning of security as peace of heart (vss. 1-8). Not a bright spot in this man's sky, or a sad note in his song.
  A. Freedom from fear by day and night
    Vs. 5 used in London during almost every blitz
  B. Calmness of heart amid sickness and pestilence
    Vs. 6 used by Daniel Defoe about the London Plague (1665)
  C. Freedom from fright in the day of battle
    Vs. 7—not freedom from peril, but peace of heart
II. The secret of security as trusting God (vss. 9-16). The secret lies with God, not with oneself or with things.
  A. Keeping close to God in faith
    Thinking about Him, referring everything to Him

B. Doing the will of God in love
C. Leaving results to God in hope
Concl.—An offer of this peace, here and now, in Christ

In this kind of sermon a man has less difficulty with the first main part than with the second. He can describe security as it appears in the psalm and in life today, but how can he lead the lay hearer to the source, in a vital experience with God? Here again the expositor can find help in biography, such as *A Man Called Peter*.[2] In Washington, D.C., at a time when her young husband, a pastor, lay hovering between two worlds, Mrs. Peter Marshall "sent an SOS to two prayer specialists." That night she went to the bedside of her six-year-old son and asked him to pray that his father might get well. At the time she knew that the medical experts thought her husband might not live until morning. What could she say when the little boy asked, "But, Mommy, will God keep His promise? Does God *always* keep His promises?" Should she say Yes, or No, or should she hedge?

"Yes, Peter, God does always keep His promises." The proof came within fifteen hours. The father recovered from that illness and went on to do the best work of his life, a life that he may have shortened by attempting to do more than one man's work. Meanwhile the wife and mother had learned the secret of inner security.

Sometimes the needed example comes from a missionary biography. If a man wishes the people to grow in missionary zeal and giving, he should saturate his soul with facts from the lives of missionaries, and then use these facts to show the spirit and the meaning of passages from the Bible. For instance, look

[2] By Catherine Marshall (New York: McGraw-Hill Book Co., 1951) , p. 218, *et al.*

at Ps. 107. As a whole it contains more truths than one may wish to use in a single message, though they all belong together. After three verses of introduction the psalm falls into four parts, each of which has to do with deliverance from peril, that is, with redemption from evil. "Redemption is the theme," writes Dr. Kyle M. Yates. Then he points out four pictures:

GOD SEES AND HEARS

I. Redemption for the lost ones (vss. 4-9)
II. Redemption for the bound ones (vss. 10-16)
III. Redemption for the afflicted ones (vss. 17-22)
IV. Redemption for the storm-tossed ones (vss. 23-32) [3]

Another interpreter would stress the two refrains that ring out through the psalm, each of them four times. The first refrain, "They cried to the Lord in their trouble, and he delivered them from their distress." The second refrain, "Let them thank the Lord for his steadfast love, for his wonderful works to the sons of men!"

Still another plan would call for a message from vss. 23-32 about deliverance from fear during a storm at sea. Strange as it may seem, people who live far inland, and never have seen an ocean or a seagoing ship, feel much concern about this record of a storm at sea. They also like to hear about Alexander Duff, one of the most scholarly young missionaries who ever went forth from Scotland.[4] In 1829 at the age of twenty-three, after a brilliant record at the university, he and his bride sailed out to India, where he was to serve as the first missionary of his Church. Twice the wooden vessel encountered terrific storms. The second time, as it drew near to the Cape of Good Hope,

---

[3] See *Preaching from the Psalms* (New York: Harper & Bros., 1948) , pp. 144-53.
[4] See George Smith, *The Life of Alexander Duff* (London: Hodder & Stoughton, 1881) , pp. 48-49.

the ship was beaten to pieces on the rocks. Every person on board was spared, but not without the loss of all possessions. Duff and his bride lost all their earthly goods, including the eight hundred books that he had carefully chosen for work among the young scholars of India.

On the shore a sailor found Duff's Bible and hymnbook, or Psalter, wrapped up in a waterproof cloth. Gathering about him on the shore the survivors of the storm, both passengers and members of the crew, Duff led them in a service of praise. First of all, knowing the Book of Psalms, he read these verses about the way the Lord God watches over His people amid the worst of storms at sea. Then he led in a prayer of thanksgiving and committed everyone to God for freedom "from all ills, in this world and the next." "Oh that men would praise the Lord for his goodness, and for his wonderful works to the children of men!" (K.J.V.)

5. EMPLOYING FACTS FROM LIFE TODAY

The more difficult the passage, the more need of facts from life today. Now we turn to perhaps the most difficult of all psalms, the 139th. The difficulty springs partly from our present-day fashion of interpreting a Bible passage impersonally and abstractly instead of simply trying to explain what it says and what it means in fact forms of our day. Because of learned treatises about the Psalms we read into this one our impersonal scholastic abstractions about Omniscience, Omnipresence, Omnipotence, and Transcendence. All true, but sadly different from the simple words of the psalm with its matchless beauty and power. The difficulty comes to its height in the latter part of the song, which most interpreters pass by without comment. Even in these closing verses the words of the old-time bard may have a message for every hearer today.

Light on the psalm comes from James Denney, at Glasgow, master theologian of yesterday. In a volume of strong sermons[5] he begins with a discussion of the 139th psalm as a whole. The Scottish divine insists that even in the Book of Psalms this one has "an eminence of its own." It deals with "the soul's direct and overwhelming experience of God." In the song "there is nothing about omniscience." "The important thing in religion is not the belief that God is omniscient, but the experience that God knows me." "The important thing is not . . . that God is everywhere, but that . . . wherever I am, God is with me." Every man's "being has its ground in God." He is the Source of the distinction "between right and wrong." From this lofty point of view let us look at the psalm, with the opening verse as the keynote, "O Lord, thou hast searched me."

Your Soul Under the Searchlight

Everyone stands in awe before Ps. 139.
Here your soul passes under God's searchlight.
I. God knows you just as you are (vss. 1-6). The Celestial Surgeon as your Friend
    A. Everything good He sees and blesses.
    B. Everything evil He wishes to remove.
II. God goes with you wherever you go (vss. 7-12). The Divine Companion, not "the hound of heaven."
    A. He never lets you escape from His presence.
    B. He longs to bless you as you flee.
III. God has made you what you are (vss. 13-18). The Divine Artist, and His masterpiece.
    A. Apart from sin, your being has come from God.
    B. Gratefully accept your personality as His gift.
IV. God wants you to battle on His side (vss. 19-24). The Divine Crusader, and His Holy War
    A. He is engaged in a campaign against evil.

[5] *The Way Everlasting* (London: Hodder & Stoughton, 1911), pp. 1-12. Used by permission.

B. He wishes you to enlist and fight.
Under the searchlight of God a man feels his need of the Cross.

The fourth main section (vss. 19-24) bristles with difficulties. On the other hand, if one takes up this closing section and tries to show what it means for a man today, one can answer some of the layman's questions. "Why should the psalmist talk about hating his foes?" As Denney says, "How . . . can a soul which has been flooded with the consciousness of God, of His intimate nearness, of His all-penetrating love, how can such a soul be overcome by such a temper? Surely these are not pious prayers." Let the sage of Glasgow answer his own question:

I cannot think that in a mind so great as that of the writer of this Psalm—and . . . in a work of art so perfect—there should be an unprovoked and sudden lapse into mere inconsistency. There must be a connexion . . . between these passionate words and what precedes, and I believe it is not hard to find. . . . [The psalmist] knows . . . that what is going on in the world is a battle, and that it is the Lord's battle, and that it is vital to be on the Lord's side. . . . The Cross of Christ, where He died for the difference between right and wrong, . . . teaches the same truth as the vehement Psalmist, and makes the same appeal. "Who is on the Lord's side?" it calls to us as we look out upon life. And it is only as we enlist under that ensign, and commit ourselves to fight the good fight to the last, that we can share in the experiences which inspired this wonderful Psalm.[6]

In full view of all its difficulties one of our sons not long ago preached from Ps. 139 as a whole. He knew that his most thoughtful laymen felt puzzled about the meaning of the psalm when they used it as a responsive reading. In the sermon,

[6] *Ibid.,* pp. 9, 11.

without evasion or apology, he took up the four main sections and tried to translate the ideas into thought forms of that county-seat congregation. Afterward the people spoke to his parents more appreciatively about that message than about any other all year. They admired the courage of the young man in facing this difficult undertaking, and they appreciated his ability to make the psalm seem helpful today. Most of all, they felt grateful for new light on what it means for a man to have religion, or rather, for God to have His way in the heart of His servant.

For the warp of a message the psalm provides abundance of materials, more than anyone can use in a sermon no longer than twenty-five minutes. As for the woof, anyone can find in the psalm all sorts of leads out into life today. For example, think of the fluoroscope in the hands of an expert in diagnosing diseases of the chest. A sense of relief comes when the specialist assures a man of middle age that his heart and his lungs are sound and free from disease. Searching of soul begins if the specialist discovers marks of infection or injury. In either event, the patient looks on the wise man of science as a friend and benefactor.

The second part of the psalm leads the interpreter to think in terms of travel. It may be a journey by air, as one ascends up into the heavens and wings one's way to the ends of the earth. The travel may come by proxy, as one sits at home and reads about the adventures of Osa Helen Johnson in her expeditions to Africa for a study of cannibals and wild life in the jungle. "Oh, if I could travel! If I could only see the Holy Land and the Passion Play!" Peace, dear heart, you would have to take yourself along. Even while sitting at home, you can learn from Ps. 139 the inner meaning of restfulness.

The third part takes the interpreter into the realm of psychology and leads him to think much about such present-day concerns as physique and temperament, though not in these prosaic terms.[7] The closing verses call for thoughts about life as a crusade, which Bunyan would term a "Holy War." In the psalm as a whole think about God as the Prime Mover—as Surgeon, as Companion, as Creator, and as Warrior. Think of Him in the everyday experience of the friend in the pew.[8] Does the psalm bring the man in the pew a sense of serenity and up-lift, or a feeling of unrest and fear? That depends on how the hearer looks upon God and responds to a sense of His presence. A man may even want to flee.

One of the ablest living theologians has published a sermon about Ps. 139 under the heading, "Man's Escape from God." The message contains many excellent ideas, all of them in keeping with the passage. Man today does try to escape from God. He does not wish to have the secrets of his heart revealed, but he finds that he cannot hide from the Most High. So there is in man today a tension, a struggle, for which the psalm provides a remedy. In full view of life about us, with all of its wickedness, let us turn to God in prayer. The conclusion of the semiphilosophical sermon, like much that precedes, has to do with "all men."

Despite its depth of insight and its power of thought, this kind of treatment might leave the lay hearer unsatisfied and cold. Would it not prove better to let the psalm speak for itself? It exalts God, not us. It deals with one person, not with men. Man is an abstract term, and, as Denney points out, "abstract

[7] See Wm. H. Sheldon, *The Varieties of Human Physique* (New York: Harper & Bros., 1940) ; also, *The Varieties of Temperament* (New York: Harper & Bros., 1942).

[8] See W. E. Hocking, *The Meaning of God in Human Experience* (New Haven: Yale University Press, 1912).

nouns are unequal to the intense feeling of the passage." The psalm deals with the subject positively. It stresses the fact of God in the experience of a man like the one yonder in the pew. Indeed, the psalm points to this friend himself. So should the sermon. In short, take the strong ideas of the song and translate them into terms of a layman's experience today. By so doing you can come close to the heart of Ps. 139, and closer still to the heart of God as the Supreme Transformer.

There is nothing new about these two ways of preaching. For present purposes we may refer to them as the factual and the philosophical. No doubt each of them has its place. In popular expository preaching, as a rule, the factual method proves far more interesting and helpful to the average hearer. The distinction between the two ways of speaking appears in words from Cicero, who wrote about fifty years before the birth of Christ. While the present-day expositor ought not to think of himself as an orator, he should take these sayings to heart. Then he will strive to make his pulpit work as full of facts and person-centered as the 139th psalm.

It is the business of an orator to speak in a manner adapted to persuade. . . . Every speech is either upon a question concerning a matter in general, without specification of persons and times, or concerning a matter referring to certain persons and times.[9]

6. PREFERRING FACTS ABOUT ONE PERSON

In the use of facts give the preference to those that relate to one person of interest to the hearer. Testimony to this effect comes from an expert who has devoted his life to welfare work

[9] See *Cicero on Oratory and Orators*, transl. and ed. by J. S. Watson (London, 1884), p. 177. See also P. T. Forsyth, *Positive Preaching and the Modern Mind* (New York: Hodder & Stoughton, 1907), pp. 3-5.

among the world's unfortunates, especially the lepers. His moving novel about them, *Who Walk Alone* (1940), shows the meaning of the Gospel in action. More recently this expert has written a less moving autobiography in which he tells the secret of raising money for lepers and for other large philanthropic causes:

> During those early fund-raising campaigns I learned that a generality—the concept of an impoverished old age, for instance— had no special meaning to people who are for the most part insulated by an "It-can't-happen-to-me" attitude. In order to bring home any situation it had to be dramatized in a single individual.[10]

In other words, this expert in raising money bids us go back to the ways of our Lord in His parables, and elsewhere in His recorded teachings. If further evidence is needed, it comes from one of the ablest modern books about preaching. "The Need for Concreteness" heads one of these chapters by a foremost theologian, Dr. H. H. Farmer, of Cambridge University. As a master of philosophy he insists that "preaching is essentially a pastoral activity." You cannot preach well to people unless you know them and love them, one by one, whatever the cost. He pleads for the use of concrete facts about persons, because our God is "the God of Detail." He is concerned about persons, one by one.

> Abstractness in some ways is the greatest curse of all our preaching. . . . The reason why the dealer in abstractions is bound to be a failure is not always understood. The reason usually given is that if we are too abstract people will not understand us, or will be uninterested and bored. There is no doubt a great deal in that,

[10] See Perry Burgess, *Born of Those Years* (New York: Henry Holt & Co., 1951), pp. 21, 22.

75

but there is a deeper reason, a reason which would hold you even if you did succeed in making your abstract statements both intelligible and interesting, the reason just given, namely that God comes at people not through abstractions at all, but through persons and through concrete situations of day-to-day personal life.[11]

[11] See *The Servant of the Word* (New York: Chas. Scribner's Sons, 1942), pp. 93, 94, 99-100.

CHAPTER FIVE

THE QUEST FOR THE UNIFYING TRUTH

W E COME NOW TO THE MOST DIFFICULT MATTER SO FAR, and one of the most important. How can we attain the sort of unity that distinguishes a sermon from most Sunday-school teaching? Critics of preaching say that the average expository sermon has neither beginning, middle, nor end. Like a ball of twine it simply unwinds. The method calls for a verse-by-verse discussion of subjects more or less interesting but apparently not related. In an extreme case an expository discourse comprises four or five sermonettes, loosely strung together, with no more apparent connection than among the islands in an archipelago, or among the stars in Ursa Minor. In preaching worthy of the name, as every student of the subject knows, each sermon has a central axis ridge that binds the whole into a single unit. Now for the question: How can we achieve and ensure unity in every expository sermon, the sort of unity that appears in every preaching passage?

In dealing with this difficult subject we may draw our cases from a difficult book, that of Judges. Let us assume that it has to do with "God's Leaders in Times of Chaos," and that it all points to the key verse at the end. "In those days there was no king in Israel; every man did what was right in his own eyes" (21:25). In chaotic times most men do wrong. Why? Partly because of a dearth in strong leadership. This holds true in many parts of the world today, and not least in our homeland. Any minister who studies the Book of Judges, despite all its difficulties, will find in it a series of dramatic scenes calling for sermons in line with the needs of our day. Here we shall consider passages that show various ways of ensuring sermonic oneness.

1. SINGLING OUT A SPECIFIC AIM

First of all, secure unity by setting up a definite goal for each sermon. "Wanted: Another Protestant Reformation." Some such statement in terms of today would bring out the preaching values in Judg. 2:11-15. Better still, "God's Call for a Revival in America" would show the present-day meaning of Judg. 3:7-11. The two passages are much alike, showing in Judges the value of repetition for emphasis. Hence we need to consider only the second. It reminds us that Old Testament history, like our own, consists largely in records of declension and revival. In recent years, around the world, we have witnessed much in the way of moral declension but little in the form of religious revival, in the biblical sense of that abused word. The passage (3:7-11) suggests the following line of thought, and the book as a whole provides all sorts of supporting facts.

> I. The irreligion of our people (vs. 7)
> II. The indignation of our God (vs. 8)
> III. The need of our prayers (vs. 9a)
> IV. The coming of our leader (vs. 9b)
> V. The victory of our God (vss. 10-11)

In this sort of preaching a man should not appear to justify war, any more than when he has the people stand to sing "Onward, Christian Soldiers." Neither should he drag into the pulpit matters of biblical criticism, about all of which he ought to become well informed.[1] The preacher ought rather to make real and vivid the sort of conditions that call for a revival of religion, and the way in which the Lord answers prayers for revival by raising up leaders, one after another, as in the time of the book before us. What concerns us now is the need of securing sermonic unity. Otherwise there might be five isolated sermonettes: about the current collapse of conscience, the biblical meaning of God's wrath, the present-day lack of intercessory prayer, the dearth of strong leadership, and the practical work of the Holy Spirit.

How can we show the unity in such a little archipelago, or constellation? Partly by phrasing a sentence to show the aim of the sermon, and then by keeping the sentence in view, both during the days of preparation and through the time of delivery. A complete declarative sentence serves better than a topic like one of those above. "In this sermon I wish to lead the hearer to pray and work for a revival of religion, beginning here at home." As in writing a book, or in making a journey, the man who prepares a sermon ought to start by defining his objective. This he should state as clearly and specifically as he knows how. Expository sermons that occasionally appear in print fall short in this respect more often than in any other. At the very beginning such a sermon should reveal a clear objective to guide the speaker and the hearer in every step of the way toward a lofty goal.

The value of a preaching aim may appear in dealing with Judg. 5:2, the key verse of the noblest war ballad in world literature. Let us think in terms of early autumn, at a church where many people have just come home from their holidays in the mountains or at the shore. The calendar calls for a

---

[1] See Alfred E. Garvie, *The Preachers of the Church* (London: Jas. Clarke, 1926), pp. 131-45.

message about spiritual advance. Instead of speaking vaguely in "A Sermon for Rally Day," the minister finds in the fifth chapter the lead for a message about "The Ideal Church for Today," or better still, "The Church That Triumphs." As often in expository sermons, the form may follow the order of ideas in the passage. The biblical materials also may come out of the chapter, and out of the triumph about which it sings. In terms of our day, and our theme, the passage shows:

I. The church that triumphs needs strong leaders (vss. 1-11).
    A. Leaders who take the lead (vs. 2)
    B. Leaders who offer themselves willingly (vs. 9)
II. The church that triumphs needs loyal followers (vss. 12-18).
    A. Men with great searchings of heart (vss. 15-16)
    B. Men with willingness to die (vs. 18)
III. The church that triumphs needs Almighty God (vss. 19-31).
    A. The God who intervenes for his people (vss. 20-21)
    B. The One who empowers His followers

The latter part of this plan calls for explanation. In summer days of old, kings went out to battle where the Brook Kishon purred along as a tiny stream. At a season when the rains descended, that rivulet quickly became a raging torrent. The poem seems to say that the elements conspired against Sisera, so that unexpectedly all of his horses and chariots became mired in the mud. In like manner the Lord God seems to have used a wind to deliver England from the oncoming Armada (1588), and a snow in October to set Moscow free from the advancing hosts of Napoleon (1812). Since one example of the kind should make the idea clear, take one of the next two.

During World War II almost half a million Allied troops, mostly British, were trapped at Dunkirk, where they seemed certain to be wiped out, or else captured en masse. But between May 26 and June 4, 1940, the Lord so governed the weather that 338,226 men were transported across the Channel in safety. Again, during the early morning of November 8, 1942, 150,000 United States troops, with 140,000 British warriors, landed in French North Africa. That perilous undertaking was carried through with scarcely any loss of life. Why? Partly because the seas that night grew calmer, according to students of statistics, than at any time during the sixty-eight years covered by existing records. "This was the Lord's doing, and it is marvelous in our eyes" (Mark 12:11).

Now let us stop and get our bearings. What has all this to do with Rally Day? If God intervened to deliver our sons and brothers in days of war, does He not care when we beseech Him to guide us in serving the Prince of Peace? According to this passage He does so through raising up leaders who inspire, with followers who rally to their support and then persevere. All of this takes place under the guidance of the Spirit, who alone can enable the local church to triumph. If any inexperienced interpreter will form the habit of unifying every message by setting up his goal, and then keeping the goal constantly in view, he can increase his effectiveness as a preacher from the Bible. In stating the purpose of any sermon give the preference to the singular. Do not be content with "showing" a Bible truth or a Christian duty. Lead the hearer to act, in his heart. Appeal to the will, perhaps indirectly.

2. THROWING STRESS ON A KEY VERSE

Once again, secure unity by singling out and stressing a short text from the passage. The longer the passage, the more the need for a single verse as a gateway into this field. For example, take Judg. 6:11-16. One could scarcely expect the lay hearer to see and recall the entire paragraph about Gideon, but one can get him to see the idea in vs. 15a. By omitting the surrounding words one can announce this text, "Pray, Lord, how can I deliver Israel?" Out of the text in its setting comes the topic, "God's Cure for an Inferiority Complex." Both text and purpose state the problem that faces an unassuming man today when the Lord calls him to religious leadership. Instead of drawing up a list of such men in the Bible, and throughout history, why not simply deal with the problem as it concerned Gideon, and as it relates to a man like him today? Think of Gideon as the noblest of all the Lord's crusaders in that rough and bloody time.

I. The man who hears the call of God (vss. 12-14)
II. The one who shrinks from a known duty (vs. 15)
III. The Lord who cures this inferiority complex (vs. 16)

In terms of the minister's study, the passage follows the idea of thesis—antithesis—synthesis, with the last as most important. Even when translated into workaday English, the basic ideas may mean little to the man in the pew until he begins to see the meaning of his own inferiority complex. He ought to see that such a feeling is human, and that it need not prove sinful, provided a man responds to the call of the Lord and accepts the work at hand. The matter will stand out clearly if the interpreter keeps in view the key text: "Pray, Lord, how can I deliver Israel?" The answer comes from God: "I will be with you."

That key verse suggests the cause of an inferiority complex, a cause like that of other diseases in a man's soul. Note the word "I." "Why should everything depend on me?" "I cannot do that!" "I do not know how!" "I have not the strength, or the skill!" "All true, my brother, but how about God? When He calls you to perform a known duty, does He ever let you down?" Faith here means looking away from self and seeing in God the One who is able. Able to do what? Able to do whatever He wills. It may be through a man with an inferiority complex. For the outworking of the principle study the records about Gideon as a leader after he put himself into the hands of God for service. "I can do all things in him who strengthens me" (Phil. 4:13).

3. RELYING UPON A CLEAR TOPIC

To make unity trebly sure, phrase a clear topic to interpret the passage. In this kind of expository work the text and the topic work together to show the meaning of the passage and the aim of the sermon. The text embodies the central truth. The topic shows the way the interpreter intends to use this Bible truth in meeting a certain human need today. For instance, take the need for larger activity among our Christian laymen. The message may come on "Laymen's Sunday," but it would prove still more effective as part of a course from a Bible book full of dramatic action. As a point of departure use words that appear on the inside cover of a hotel Gideon Bible, under the heading, "Who are the Gideons?"

The seventh chapter of Judges shows the reason for adopting this name. Gideon was a man willing to do exactly what God wanted him to do, irrespective of his own judgment as to plans or results. . . .

OUR MOTTO. "And they stood, every man in his place, round about the camp" (Jdg. 7:21).

With this passage and this text a man could start in any one of a dozen different directions, each of which might lead to an interesting trail. Since he has a specific purpose, he should make it luminous at once by stating a clear topic. On the other hand, if he wished merely to inspire, he might do so by phrasing a topic that would suggest far more than it said. For instance, take Dr. Arthur J. Gossip's well-known book title, *The Hero in Thy Soul.* A study of sermons by master expositors, such as Maclaren and Robertson, will show that they excelled in phrasing clear topics, whereas nonexpository preachers often show the uplift of suggestive topics. Why not learn to use both kinds? But in expository work give the right of way to a teaching topic which is clear. The plan below does not follow the order of the ideas in the passage, but aims to show the use of a clear topic:

THE RELIGION OF OUR LAYMEN
   I. They need a cause large enough to call out loyalty.
  II. They need a leader strong enough to arouse enthusiasm.
 III. They need a plan bold enough to stir the imagination.
  IV. They need a God great enough to inspire faith.

Think of the Kingdom as the cause, of Christ as the Leader, of taking the community as the plan, and of God as the Giver of Faith. Faith here means human weakness laying hold on divine power to accomplish the impossible. At the end of the hour in church the lay hearer may not clearly recall every fact about Gideon and his three hundred. These facts he can find in the Bible at home, and he should feel an urge to read the passage with new understanding. Better still, he should resolve to do his full share in carrying out the spirit of the pastor's message about "The Religion of Our Laymen."

After a discourse of another kind, inspirational rather than informative, a pastor in a large city made a moving plea for laymen to volunteer. Echoing John Wesley, the minister said in substance: "If I had three hundred men completely dedicated to Christ and His Church, I could bring the Kingdom of God into our city."

At the end of the service one of the laymen in that large congregation came forward to thank the minister for his inspiring message, and also to volunteer. "Pastor, I think I can enlist those three hundred men. What shall I tell them of your plans to capture our city for Christ?" Alas, the minister had nothing definite to propose, at least nothing bold enough to capture the imagination of a potential leader among God's laymen.[2] Surely that preacher did not employ what I call the topical method of expository pulpit work.

4. MAKING A DIRECT APPROACH

A sense of unity also depends much upon what a man puts first in the sermon. The discussion now relates to the introduction, which need not run long. A man with a teaching aim plans to introduce his subject at once. In other types of preaching, useful and uplifting, he may arouse curiosity about what he hopes to accomplish, and about the trail he expects to follow. In preaching, as in dramatic art, suspense has a worthy place. But in a teaching sermon there should from the start be no uncertainty about what the speaker has in view. Present-day psychology shows that the hearer grasps most surely and remembers most clearly what the speaker puts in the forefront.[3] Put the first thing first.

For example, think about "A Bible Fable for Voters" (Judg. 9:8-15). In other days an expositor would have begun with something about this fable in the Bible. Today an interpreter feels more inclined to start with a present human need, a need that has to do with voters. For the sake of variety, why not use both methods, the contextual and the problem

[2] For an example of a positive sort from the same city, see my *Pastoral Leadership* (New York and Nashville: Abingdon-Cokesbury Press, 1949), pp. 228-30.

[3] See F. K. Berrien, *Practical Psychology* (New York: The Macmillan Co., 1944), p. 513, "Driving to the Point." See p. 120, *infra*.

approach, but at different times? In either case the first thing to do is to help the hearer get his bearings so that he will want to follow the trail to the end, and with growing interest. Especially at a time when election day looms up ahead, everyone ought to feel concerned about this subject. If anyone does not, he surely needs the sermon. Whatever the order of presentation, the message ought to bring out these related truths: the need in our midst for voters who do the will of God at the ballot box, and the light this fable throws on the matter today. As for the sermon, it need only explain and illuminate the passage, mainly in terms of our time. Let us assume that the hearer has just listened to a skillful reading of this fable about the way the trees selected their ruler. He wants to know what the fable means today.

I. The olive tree may represent the businessman, too busy to serve his country (or city).
II. The fig tree may represent the lover of culture, too cultured to serve his country.
III. The vine may represent the lover of self, too selfish to serve his country.
IV. The bramble may represent the lover of corruption, too corrupt to serve his country.

Without some guiding topic, and back of it a controlling purpose, a man might soon get lost in the woods. By way of introduction he could talk for a while about the two fables in the Bible (cf. II Kings 14:9); the differences between a fable, a parable, and an allegory; and the difference between the fable at hand and one from Aesop. A man of a different bent could show how much he has learned from the *Encyclopaedia Britannica* about olive trees, fig trees, grapevines, and bramble bushes. A third man could hold forth on what Viscount Bryce predicted about the perils in our American cities, because of apathy among potential voters. The older a man grows, and the more widely he reads, the more he tends to distract by calling attention to related concerns, when he ought to focus on the one truth in view.

Suppose that a man has in mind the topic, "A Bible Fable for Voters." He should let it serve as a guiding beam to keep the sky pilot on his trail. Stage after stage, from the beginning of the flight until the end, he should let nothing divert him from following this guiding light. In keeping with the spirit of the fable the sermon ought to have both variety and beauty, but never at the expense of unity. The friend in the pew ought to pass through much the same experience as the preacher. "One thing I do." "During the next twenty-five minutes I want to learn all I need to know about this 'Bible Fable for Voters.'" Throughout the rest of his life the layman ought to live in the light of a fable that he did not know was in the Bible. All of this follows most surely when the man in the pulpit makes a direct approach.

5. PHRASING A DEFINITE THEME

Unity comes also through phrasing and stressing a definite theme. A "theme" here means a proposition, or key sentence, which embodies the substance of the entire sermon. In recent times the theme, or proposition, has not bulked so large as in other days, both in writings about homiletics[4] and in the actual work of preaching. Whether or not a proposition appears prominently in the spoken message, a key sentence does help to keep the speaker from wandering off into subjects not directly in line with the sermon. Of course, the proposition ought to be closely related to the aim, the text, and the topic.

[4] See Austin Phelps, *The Theory of Preaching*, rev. by F. D. Whitesell (Grand Rapids: Eerdmans Pub. Co., 1947).

For example, Judg. 13:2-8 has to do with the delicate subject of concern about an unborn baby. The time may soon come when the minister will feel free to bring out in the pulpit what the Bible says about the most important event in the life of a Godly home:

THE BIBLE ABOUT THE COMING OF A BABY

I. The spirit of the expectant mother (vss. 2-7)
II. The prayer of the expectant father (vs. 8)
III. The blessing on the expected child (vss. 24-25a)

In 1951, 3,758,000 babies were born in our land. In Christian circles everyone today shows concern about courtship and marriage, also about the training of a little child. Amen! But what about the troublesome months that lie between the conception of the child in the womb and the coming of the little one to bless the home? The Bible has more than a little to say about the wisdom of preparing the hearts of both parents for the advent of their first baby. If a minister dares to speak on the subject, perhaps before a mothers' club, he may single out this text: "O, Lord, I pray thee, let the man of God whom thou didst send [to bless us at our marriage] come again to us, and teach us what we are to do with the boy that shall be born" (13:8).

The aim is clear. In the spirit of this key verse the pastor has a mission from God to guide both expectant parents. The basic truths for his message should come out of the chapter. What of the proposition? This key sentence may stand at the very beginning of the sermon, after the minister has announced his text and his topic. In another sermon, if only for variety, the proposition may come at the end of a brief introduction. In either case the key sentence ought to sound out again and again, at intervals, to remind the hearer that everything centers around the one key thought. The proposition: "During the months before the coming of a baby, each parent ought continually to seek the guidance of God."

This kind of key sentence calls for exposition, rather than argument or defense. The pastor does not enter the pulpit as a debater or a reformer. According to George Adam Smith, master expositor, "The Bible contains singularly little argument in response to the questions it starts." Really we know little about the mental development of a babe in the womb, but we believe that God has given the little one life, and that He can prepare both father and mother for the most important and exacting privilege of all their earthly experiences together. Every father ought also to feel, with Manoah of old, that the Lord's guidance will come through the pastor of the local church.

Never should a text or a theme about childbirth lead to levity. God forbid that any interpreter of religion and life should make sport of an expectant father. One might as well make light of marriage itself, which the Bible employs as earth's noblest example of the relation between Christ and His Church.[5] When ought a young husband to feel his kinship with God more surely and strongly than during the months while he looks forward to first becoming a father? At such a time he should become well acquainted with Horace Bushnell's classic volume, *Christian Nurture*. In his sermons Bushnell often shows the value of using a proposition. In this other work he has a message for the expectant father.[6]

The child is not to have the sad entail of any sensuality, or excess, or distempered passion upon him. The heritage of love, peace,

[5] See Eph. 5:25-33, Rev. 21:2, Isa. 62:4-5, *et al.*

[6] See the latest edition edited by L. A. Weigle (New Haven: Yale University Press, 1947), II, 1, 197-98.

order, continence, and holy courage is to be his. He is not to be morally weakened beforehand, in the womb of folly, by the frivolous, worldly, ambitious expectations of parents-to-be, concentrating all their nonsense in him. His affinities are to be raised by the godly expectations, rather, and the prayers that go before. . . . Born, thus, of a parentage that is ordered in all righteousness, and maintains the right use of every thing . . . the child will have just so much of heaven's life and order in him beforehand, as have become fixed properties in the type of his parentage.

6. SETTING UP CONSPICUOUS GUIDEPOSTS

A preacher can help to ensure unity by setting up a few conspicuous guideposts. Here I shall anticipate what will appear later under the heading of structure. In preparing for any kind of popular teaching message no one can overestimate the value of a few clear landmarks, or guideposts, which stand out boldly along the winding trail. At the end of a sermon the lay follower may or may not remember these places at which he would have lost his way if the guideposts had not pointed out the trail along the upward path. Of course no seeker of pleasure needs guideposts on a merry-go-round, or on an escalator.

For the sake of clarity the expositor may follow the example of Maclaren. As we have seen, he often phrased his headings in the form of sentences. In each main heading he embodied the topic, and he made each heading conform to a pattern, known as parallelism. Occasionally, if only for sake of variety, he would let phrases take the place of sentence headings. Whatever the pattern today, both leader and follower find it easier to read the signs when they all embody the same general design. If this way of marking important crossroads sounds wooden, remember that in a sermon the guideposts appear only at intervals, and that they give everyone concerned a feeling of assurance. From this point of view consider the sixteenth chapter of Judges, with vs. 17, or vs. 20c, as the keynote:

The Temptations of a Young Athlete

Especially in the autumn almost everyone thinks about athletics. So does the Bible tell much about physical prowess. Think of Samson as the world's supreme all-round athlete. He would have carried off all the prizes at the Olympic Games.

I. A young athlete has God-given powers.
    A. Think of strength and skill as gifts from God.
    B. Note the power of such a man for service.
II. A young athlete may abuse God-given powers.
    A. This athlete of old was always strong against men.
    B. He was equally weak in the hands of a bad woman.
III. The mightiest young athlete may lose God-given powers.
    A. He finds God patient and long-suffering.
    B. But he may exhaust the patience of God.
IV. The outworn athlete may regain his lost powers.
The path of safety lies in dedicating your body to God.

Few questions are graver for a man than the character of the woman to whose influence he voluntarily surrenders himself. Few questions are graver for a woman than the character of the influence she permits herself to exert upon a man. Nothing is more noteworthy in this history than the illustration it affords of the difference between physical and moral courage.[7]

The facts about Samson raise another problem, ethical rather than homiletical. Through the years pastors of various schools—such as Spurgeon and Brooks, or Chappell and Macartney—have preached about Samson and Delilah. The first three of the above-mentioned pastors have held up Samson, before his debacle, as an example of consecration. This seems out of keeping with the facts in the Bible, and with the needs

[7] See Canon H. P. Liddon, *Sermons at St. Paul's Cathedral* (London, 1886), "Lessons from the Life of Samson," p. 134.

of our day. Let Samson serve as a living example of the way God may endow a man with powers almost superhuman, and of the way a mighty athlete may abuse his powers until at last he loses them. Where in the Book of Judges can any Christian minister point to a single fact about Samson as an object lesson of what it means to be holy in body and heart?

The records in Judges lead to a still more difficult and important question which relates to doctrine. The Apostle once wrote about the Hebrew Bible, "All Scripture is inspired by God and profitable" (II Tim. 3:16a; see vss. 15-17.) Did he mean to include Judg. 16 and the next five chapters? Evidently he did. Where in classic literature can anyone find much more of blood and filth? How then inspired? As warnings. As danger signals. Here stand out the traits of human nature, "red in tooth and claw." The Scriptures are profitable for what? "For reproof, for correction, for training in righteousness." Without professing to have solved other problems here, let us frankly acknowledge that the Bible would not seem complete without records like these in the latter part of Judges. Let us help the lay reader of the Holy Scriptures to interpret them intelligently. Let us also rejoice that in the same volume with the Book of Judges we have the Gospel According to John. Is all this Bible inspired? Yes. Is it profitable? Yes. But it is not all equally inspiring and not all equally profitable, or in the same fashion. None of it will seem inspiring and profitable unless it is understood. "As for him who is sown 'on good soil,' that is the man who hears the word and understands it; he bears fruit" (Matt. 13:23, Moffatt).

7. RELYING ON CAREFUL REPETITION

Unity may likewise come through intelligent repetition. The principle of repetition appears everywhere in the present chapter about unity. The successive parts of the discussion endeavor to show that a minister ought to use every means at his command to bring out the oneness of the Bible passage and of the resulting sermon. He wishes the main parts of the message to stand out as boldly as the piers of a suspension bridge.[8] Like a builder of bridges, the man who makes a sermon ought to think of each structure as a whole. He should ever keep in view the controlling purpose, to lead the hearer safely from where he is to where he ought to be. Instead of feeling obliged to put into the construction all of the stones he finds in a biblical quarry, he should select and omit. Throughout the entire structure he keeps repeating the same motif. As in a bridge, all of the piers look alike. By way of confirmation listen to one of the wisest men who have lectured at Yale:

Never be afraid of saying the same thing over and over again, if you feel driven to say it by a strong sense of its importance. . . . Young preachers are afraid to say the same thing over and over again. . . . We should all preach more effectively if, instead of taxing our intellectual resources to say a great many things in the same sermon, we tried to say a very few things in a great many ways.[9]

On the other hand, repetition for its own sake may quickly become monotonous, if not ridiculous. It may cause the hearer to suspect, rightfully, that a minister has run out of anything more to say, and that he must keep repeating what seemed scarcely worth saying the first time. A minister need never incur such suspicions after he has mastered any preaching unit in the Bible and then has planned to present these truths in a fitting garb. "Familiarity breeds contempt" only

[8] See D. B. Steinman, *The Builders of the Bridge* (New York: Harcourt, Brace & Co., 1945).

[9] See Robert W. Dale, *Nine Lectures on Preaching* (New York: George H. Doran Co., 1878), pp. 122, 149-50.

when a man deals with contemptible things, and in a contemptible manner. As a lover of sermons, all sorts of sermons, I always find it difficult to name any present-day master of the preacher's art who has not learned the value of meaningful repetition.

A wise man does not Sunday after Sunday repeat himself in the same old ways, old to his hearers. In that case a certain preacher would become known for always harping on his text, another on his topic, a third on his proposition, and a fourth on his headings. Why not cultivate wholesome variety, such as you find in Holy Writ? No book on earth contains more in the way of both repetition and variety. Phrase with special care, and repeat at intervals, whatever you wish the hearer to remember. Do not expect him to remember everything, but take pains that he will remember something, if only enough to tell his wife at home in bed with her firstborn daughter. Better still, send him home with something glowing in his soul. Among all these counsels about the wisdom of seeking variety, permit one exception. Whatever you stress, or do not stress, always leave in the hearer's mind an illuminated text as the keynote of the sermon.

Why so much insistence on variety? Because expository preachers and sermons, rightly or wrongly, have become known for tameness, sameness, and lameness. In content they are often admirable, in form perhaps satisfactory, but week after week increasingly monotonous—as much alike as automobiles on an assembly line. If so, the preacher must lack imagination. In no two of the Bible passages at which we have glanced can anyone find the same sort of materials or the same kind of moving spirit. If any two of the resulting sermons seem much alike, at least one of them misrepresents its passage. What a fearful thing for a full-time ordained interpreter to stand up in the pulpit and misrepresent any part of God's Written Word!

A much more important question relates to unity. Why all this insistence on the oneness of every sermon? Facetiously, why not go "everywhere preaching the gospel"? For various reasons, notably four. Since each of them ought to seem self-evident, let me merely state them, with little comment.

1. *The Biblical.* Every preaching passage in Holy Writ has at heart a unifying truth. Not to bring out the central message would mean to misrepresent a certain part of God's Written Word. Then the sermon might seem like a valley full of dead men's bones, very many and dry.[10]

2. *The Historical.* In the past every expositor worthy of the name has excelled in the sort of synthesis that sees a truth or a duty in the large, and sees it as a whole. Not to do so now would show a man's unworthiness to wear the mantle of any expository hero.

3. *The Contemporary.* Expository preaching currently has gone out of favor largely because of weakness or failure at this point. According to Charles E. Jefferson, a master of the preacher's art, "an aimless sermon breaks down the interest of a congregation and sends it home disheartened and confused." [11]

4. *The Pastoral.* A so-called sermon without a unified message does not meet the needs of men today. When they come to church out of a world full of chaos and fear, they need a sermon where the Spirit of God comes into a valley full of dead men's bones and makes them live.

"So I prophesied [or preached] as he commanded me, and

[10] See the mighty preaching passage, Ezek. 37:1-10.

[11] See *Quiet Hints to Growing Preachers* (New York: T. Y. Crowell Co., 1901), p. 87, "The Value of a Target."

the breath came into them, and they lived, and stood upon their feet, an exceedingly great host" (Ezek. 37:10). Homiletically, the same truth may sound forth from a martial hymn dear to the hearts of churchgoers. Here let it apply to the parts of a sermon, marching on to victory, like an army with flying banners:

> We are not divided,
> All one body we,
> One in hope and doctrine,
> One in charity.[12]

[12] From "Onward, Christian Soldiers" (1865), by S. Baring-Gould.

CHAPTER SIX

THE VARIETIES OF SERMON STRUCTURE

LIKE EVERY OTHER SORT OF PULPIT TEACHING, AN expository sermon calls for structure. If a minister wishes not to teach so much as to inspire, he may give less heed to making a sturdy framework. In a message intended to uplift, careful structure may not be essential, but even there it can do no harm, especially if it calls no attention to itself. When a man enters the pulpit to teach, in ways most appealing, he ought to proceed clearly from stage to stage. Why so? Partly because he finds basic structure in every teaching passage of the Book. For example, think about the parables of our Lord, first in Matthew. Note that each of them has the sort of oneness and order, symmetry and progress, which mark the structure of any first-class piece of writing or speaking intended to instruct. As we look at some of the parables in the First Gospel, the principles about structure should emerge. Among them let us note the varieties of framework. In other passages we should find still different ways of putting things together, but we need not go beyond the parables in Matthew.

1. CONTRASTING THE GOOD AND THE BAD

Our Lord loved to teach by voicing a positive idea and then a negative. Again and again He presented truths in this order. As a rule He pointed to one person at a time. For instance, take the well-known sermon-story at the end of the

"Teaching on the Hill." In the parable about the two houses, first the Master Teacher shows the ideal, as it concerns a man like the one who listens. Then by contrast He brings out the actual, again like a man whom the Teacher addresses. All this is in terms of building a house that the hearer may consider as a home for his wife and little ones. The parable shows the blending of what a German scholar terms "popular intelligibility and impressive pregnancy." With amusing absence of the simplicity that he praises, the savant points out "two weighty qualities" in the parables of our Lord.

The importance lies in the union of these two qualities. A mode of teaching which aims at popular intelligibility is exposed to the risk of degenerating into platitude and triviality; and one which aims at pregnant brevity easily becomes stilted and obscure. But Jesus perfectly combined the two qualities, and by this very means attained a peculiar and classic beauty.[1]

He did so not least by the use of structure, as in the parable at hand (Matt. 7:24-27). The word religion in the topic below means Christianity at work.

A Man's Religion in Terms of Building

Everyone likes to watch a building going up.
In early manhood our Lord served as a builder.
He tells a man how to make the most of his life.
   I. The house on the rock shows the ideal. What the Lord wishes every man to do.
      A. The foundation, the basis—get right with God
      B. The rising walls—get right with others
      C. The storm, a time of testing—get right with self
   II. The house on the sand shows the actual. What a man does with his life, apart from God.

[1] See Hans Hinrich Wendt, *The Teaching of Jesus,* 2 vols. (New York: Chas. Scribner's Sons, 1896) , I, 109.

A. No foundation—to ensure stability in a storm
B. No right relations—to ensure usefulness
C. No inner strength—to withstand a tempest

All of this our Lord shows pictorially rather than prosaically, as it appears above. In dealing with the two houses He employs a sort of parallelism well known to hearers versed in the Old Testament. Almost word for word He pictures the second building as like the first in every respect save the foundation. The truth of the sermon-story all centers in contrast. Contrast is only another name for the kind of structure that we associate with F. W. Robertson. He learned it from his Lord. How can any interpreter today deal fairly with the parable unless he shows the contrast between the two builders, and in the Master's order? Who would try to "improve" on this masterpiece from the hand of the Supreme Artist? Alas, most of us would either have a three-point sermon or else put the house on the sand before the one on the rock.

If a man follows his Master Teacher and deals first with the positive half of the sermon-story, he should have no difficulty in making the truth clear. If he wishes to avoid "degenerating into platitude and triviality," he may use an illustration from engineering. In 1900 a tidal wave from the West Indies swept across the Gulf of Mexico and almost submerged the city of Galveston, leaving about five thousand persons dead and untold millions of dollars worth of property destroyed. Before the mud had dried in the streets, the city fathers determined to build a wall so strong and so high that never again would the city face impending doom. They secured the best engineer they could find, and instructed him to build a wall as mighty as the Rock of Gibraltar.

A few years later, according to reports, the engineer who had erected the wall at Galveston was engaged on a gigantic enterprise in Alaska. One day he received a telegram saying that another tidal wave had swept over the gulf and demolished his wall. Handing the telegram to an assistant engineer, the chief said with a smile, "Somebody has made a mistake. I built that wall to stand." So it proved. Today that wall still stands, with a strength like that in the Rock of Ages.

The difficulty, homiletically, comes with the second half of the sermon. If a man finds it hard to keep away from banality in dealing with the truth positively, how can he keep from anticlimax when he covers the same ground the second time? Of course he knows that the hearer feels far more concern about the house that collapses during a storm than about the one that stands for a hundred years. Even so, the latter half of the sermon calls for superb craftsmanship, lest a man merely elaborate the obvious. One way to avoid the difficulty would be to deal with the parable—the first part of it—much as in the plan above. Then in the latter part of the sermon show how the negative idea works in a few cases, more or less typical.

Phillips Brooks often preached this way. In all his ten volumes, with two hundred sermons,[2] he did not use this parable. If he had done so, he would first have made clear the meaning of his passage. Then he might have singled out three or four persons, each of them imaginary, but like someone in Boston, to show the meaning of the truth in view. For instance, think of a young fellow facing marriage. The man in the pulpit would address his young friend kindly, yet with searchings of heart. "Are you planning to build your new home on the foundation of faith in God? If not, the house will fall." Next comes a student in college with his eyes fixed

[2] See *Phillips Brooks's Sermons* (New York: E. P. Dutton & Co., 1910).

on a brilliant career, and then a merchant trying to succeed in business while ignoring God.

This way of developing a truth by the use of cases from life proves so easy and so fascinating that a man may feel tempted to multiply his examples. Before he gets through he may wander far from the parable and try indirectly to explain Arnold J. Toynbee's *Study of History*, or P. A. Sorokin's *Crisis of Our Age*, with a sociological diagnosis of "our sensate civilization." Would it not be better to follow the Master, as well as Brooks, and keep to the sort of person who lives across the street?

Once again, an example from engineering may help to bring out the meaning of the parable, this time negatively. Ordinarily we think of a church as built upon a rock, but even a church edifice may fall. In Boston, as every visitor ought to know, the Back Bay District consists of man-made land. In the older days engineers took the top off Beacon Hill and carried the soil out into the Back Bay. On that sort of ground you can erect smaller buildings but not a massive church. According to tradition, a certain congregation erected in the Back Bay area an edifice with beauty and charm, both without and within. Soon after the people began to worship in the new sanctuary the trustees became concerned about cracks in the walls, cracks that kept increasing.

Wisely these laymen called in an engineer and asked him how they could make the building safe. He is said to have told them: "Gentlemen, tear down this building and dig up the foundation. Then drive steel piles down through the man-made land until you reach solid rock. You cannot build a structure like this on foundation soil that men have made."

2. POINTING OUT THE BAD AND THE GOOD

In His parables, as everywhere else, the Lord Jesus used various ways of teaching. Structurally He sometimes put the negative before the positive. Apparently He followed a simple rule: Put in the forefront what you wish the hearer to remember most clearly. In the parable about the four kinds of soil, for instance, He wishes everyone to see the folly of not receiving the Gospel aright. In this parable (Matt. 13:1-9), as every reader knows, the stress falls on the condition of the soil, not on the sower or the seed. Even when the Lord Christ preaches a sermon, and in it brings the Word of Life, the extent of the harvest depends on the hearts of the hearers. Throughout the parable the seed is the Word, or the Gospel. In each part of the tale as it unfolds, the soil is the same chemically. In the first three areas of the farm, or garden, the soil has not been properly prepared.

This interpretation appears in what our Lord told His disciples about the parable (Matt. 13:10-23). Contrary to popular opinion today, Christ's parables are not always easy to understand, but in this case we may omit the difficult part of the passage. The time available for a sermon allows a man to deal only with the main parable. For this reason he may not even read the intervening verses (10-17) about the difficulties involved. Rather let him fix attention on "Religion in Terms of Farming." In a community where people know little about country life, use "Religion in Terms of Gardening," or else "The Gospel from the Garden." In order to prepare the sermon a man needs to refresh his recollections about the Holy Land and its ways of farming.[3] Otherwise

[3] See George Adam Smith, *Historical Geography of the Holy Land* (2nd ed.; London: Hodder & Stoughton, 1936); Alfred Edersheim, *The Life and Times of Jesus the Messiah* (Chicago: W. P. Blessing Co., n.d.).

how could he explain the "rocky ground" to his congregation?

I. The beaten path shows the hearer who does not hear.
   A. The seed that never enters the soil
   B. The "Don't Care Hearer" present only in body
II. The rocky soil shows the hearer who does not think.
   A. The thin layer of soil over a sub-stratum of rock
   B. The "Hallelujah Hearer" who quickly forgets
III. The thorny soil shows the hearer who does not heed.
   A. The best of soil infested with thorns
   B. The "Too Busy Hearer" who soon loses interest
IV. The good ground shows the hearer who really hears.
   A. The bountiful return from all the seed
   B. The "I See Hearer" who pleases the Lord—this one understands (13:23).

So much for the meaning of the parable, but where is the Gospel? It should appear in the discussion, which may proceed by the use of cases. After a man has assembled a number of cases, from biography and from life today, he may find that he has an adult or two in connection with each of the first three parts, and a child of tender years with the last part. For instance, when Helen Keller was ten years of age, her father asked Phillips Brooks to tell her about God. Gladly he did so, and the two corresponded as long as he lived. Brooks was "profoundly impressed with the remark she made after the first conversation, that she had always known there was a God, but had not before known His name." In one of his later letters he told her, "The reason why we love our friends is because God loves us." [4]

A contrasting picture comes from Russia. A teacher of scientific agriculture employs the project method in dealing with a small group of boys about ten years of age. To each

[4] See A. V. G. Allen, *Life and Letters of Phillips Brooks,* 3 vols. (New York: E. P. Dutton & Co., 1901), III, 390.

lad the man in charge assigns a little plot of ground. He tells the boy to plant one half of his wee garden and care for it, always under the eye of the teacher. The other half of the plot the boy in charge must leave strictly alone. Later in the summer the teacher points out the reason for the experiment. Not only does it show that the amount of the harvest depends on the state of the soil. With subtle lack of logic the atheistic teacher points out, "You see what large crops you get when you follow the laws of Science, and how many weeds you have when you leave everything to God." For years to come we Christians must deal with the fruitage from such fiendish misuse of the project method.

3. COMPARING TWO MEN OF FORTUNE

Sometimes our Lord teaches by a contrast between one positive and another. Later in the thirteenth chapter he does so with two little parables, or "parable-germs" (vss. 44-46). Both have to do with "The Gospel in Terms of Treasure." Note the contrast. In the first case a man stumbles on hidden treasure for which he has not been seeking. In the other case a man finds treasure which he has long sought. The Master does not commend the first man for gaining possession of the treasure by purchasing the field. Like almost every other parable, or "parable-germ," this one teaches a single lesson. It shows the untold value of the Gospel, so that a wise man gives up everything in order to secure the treasure beyond price.

To a reader of the Bible and a lover of biography, living examples come to mind. Think of Jacob at Peniel, finding the God from whom he has fled. Think about Saul of Tarsus on the road to Damascus as a persecutor of the saints, and all at once finding his Saviour. Think of young Wilfred Grenfell at one of Moody's meetings in London. The medical student went to that meeting because of curiosity, and there he found the treasure that led him to change his entire career. In works of imagination turn to "The Hound of Heaven," by Francis Thompson, a poem about a man who found the One from whom he fled. Turn to "The Everlasting Mercy," by John Masefield. Here Saul Kane, a drunken wretch no longer young, finds the One who alone can transform his life. To be more accurate, each example shows that the seeker has first been sought of God, but that is not the truth in view just now.

In the companion "parable-germ" the merchant finds what he has been seeking, the "pearl of great value." Here again examples come to mind, though not as a rule so striking. The followers of John the Baptist—young men like Andrew and Peter—find the One for whom their hearts have been yearning. So does Zaccheus, and apparently Nicodemus. In the Book of Acts the Ethiopian eunuch discovers the Saviour for whom he has been searching. So does Lydia at Philippi. To run through any such list of names without the use of facts would not seem wise. Unless the people know the Bible and other classic litera- ture, these allusions would not prove clear or interesting. How- ever, a case or two, unfolded more fully, would make clear each of the contrasting truths. These two "parable-germs" should encourage the pastor to expect conversions among two sorts of men, the nonseekers and the seekers. These ought to include almost everybody.

4. CONTRASTING THE DIVINE AND THE HUMAN

Again, the contrast may concern the divine and the human, in this order. The parable about "The Forgiveness of Wrongs" (Matt. 18:21-35) embodies a contrast different from any thus far. In terms of today the passage calls for a life situation ser- mon. As the spokesman of the apostolic band Peter asks, "Lord, how often shall my brother sin against me, and I forgive him? As many as seven times?" Our Lord replies, "I do not say to you seven times, but seventy times seven." In other words, let there be no limit to your forgiveness of the man who has done you deadly wrongs. Let your forgiveness of wrongs be like God's forgiveness of your sins. As King Arthur says to his spouse, erring Guinevere,

> Lo, I forgive thee, as Eternal God
> Forgives! [5]

The first part of the parable shows "The King Who Forgives." Out of his royal bounty he cancels a personal debt of ten thousand talents, or three million pounds (Moffatt). In the currency of our time this might mean almost forty million dollars. Someone may protest, "That sounds like an impossible debt. Nobody ever owed any king that much. No ruler on earth ever canceled such a debt." True! In the days of our Lord that sum would form a major part of the entire revenue of the government in Judea.[6] Note also that the subject does not ask to have the debt canceled. He merely pleads for time that he may pay the whole amount. To his amazement he receives forgiveness, full, free, and, as he supposes, forever.

In this hypothetical case, far beyond the realms of possibility, our Lord bids us see the enormity of the sins that God stands ready to erase. On what terms? "Without money and without price."

> 'Tis heaven alone that is given away,
> 'Tis only God may be had for the asking.

[5] See Alfred Tennyson, *Idylls of the King*, "Guinevere," ll. 541-42.

[6] See Millar Burrows, *Palestine Is Our Business* (Philadelphia: Westminster Press, 1949), p. 26.

In the contrasting scene Christ shows the sinful spirit of the man who claims God's forgiveness, "The Subject Who Refuses to Forgive." The man has had his unspeakable debt canceled, but he refuses to extend the same sort of mercy to his own creditor. Here the amount involved seems small. In our currency today a hundred denarii, or about twenty dollars, might mean almost sixty dollars. Here the creditor shows the spirit of Shylock. Everyone who loves *The Merchant of Venice* has found satisfaction in watching the overthrow of that grasping schemer.

As with other parables, some details here do not apply. In certain respects the hypothetical king does not resemble God. The resulting sermon, like the tale from which it comes, ought to bring out what Dr. H. H. Farmer calls "the improbabilities of God," and the probabilities about everybody else. Think of the way our God stands ready to wipe out all the incredible debts we have piled up against Him, and the way one of us may refuse to forgive a brother who has incurred a trifling debt. To preach this way calls for courage and tact, because almost every congregation includes a prominent layman who delights in the doctrine of God's forgiveness but declines to consider his duty toward his erring brother.

An example from a distance will show how forgiveness of wrongs ought to follow forgiveness of sins. At a summer Bible conference many of us have known Bakumba, an African Negress with an angelic face and a misshapen body. Soon after her birth in the Belgian Congo the father became a Christian. Then he had to give up all his wives except the mother of Bakumba. Moved by jealous hatred, one of the former wives stole into the tent of Bakumba's mother and tried to kill the sleeping babe, succeeding only in maiming her for life. In the course of years Bakumba became a Christian, and so did her would-be murderess. At the Lord's Supper the crippled girl used to sit between her mother and the would-be murderess. Why did the daughter and her mother forgive the deadliest of wrongs? For the sake of Christ and His Cross. "Forgive us our debts, as we also have forgiven our debtors" (Matt. 6:12).

5. DEALING WITH A PROBLEM AND A SOLUTION

The Master also taught by stating a problem and then giving the solution. In like manner a pastor now may preach about problems. For one of many Bible examples he may turn to the parable about "The Laborers in the Vineyard" (Matt. 20:1-16). Here our Lord raises a problem the solution of which will tax the powers of any interpreter. In order to make the situation clear one may deal first with the sermon-story itself, and then with the meaning for our times. Thus far we have been thinking mainly about letting the form of the passage determine the structure of the sermon. There is no law to this effect, but the method would work fairly well with the parable in hand.

OUR LORD'S TREATMENT OF HIS LABORERS

Our Lord knows how much men think about money.
He uses money in teaching about the Kingdom.
I. The Lord's employment of His laborers (vss. 1-7)
   A. Those coming early represent boys and girls.
   B. The next group represents young people.
   C. The third group represents mature men and women.
   D. The fourth group represents elderly folk.
II. The Lord's payment of His laborers (vss. 8-16). The denarius, the customary wage for a day laborer.
   A. The fact that everyone receives the same amount
   B. The reason the early comers expect more
   C. The answer of the employer to these complaints
   D. The character of our God

This would provide an easy place to stop. "Have I not dealt with the parable as a whole, and with its meaning?" Yes, but what about the unspoken question in the heart of the friend in the pew? "Is such a scale of payment fair?" Why not devote the first half of the message to the parable, as above, making clear the interpretation? Then deal frankly and fully with the question. Make clear that our Lord does not here teach economics. If He did, He would seem to sanction a twelve-hour day. All through His earthly career Christ showed concern for God's suffering poor, especially for those who must toil with their hands, only to receive a pittance. By His Spirit our Lord seems to have led John Ruskin to use this passage as the basis of his book, *Unto This Last,* a moving plea for the underprivileged.[7]

In the parable at hand the Master Teacher wishes to show still more about "the improbabilities of God." The Heavenly Father deals with His redeemed children on the principle of grace. To every one He accords the strictest justice. He carries out His contract, and then He goes far beyond. He does justice, but He delights in mercy. The central truth of the parable comes close to the heart of all Christian doctrine. Some of us entered His service in the beauty of life's morning. We may feel that we have "borne the burden of the day and the scorching heat." How shall we act when we learn that the Lord of life's vineyard plans to give the very same sort of heavenly reward to those who have entered His service not long before "sunset and evening star"?[8] As children of God, let us rejoice in His grace, which is the best thing we know about God. Let

---

[7] *Unto This Last: Four Essays on the First Principles of Political Economy* (New York: John Wiley & Sons, 1867).

[8] See Maves and Cedarleaf, *Older People and the Church* (New York and Nashville: Abingdon-Cokesbury Press, 1949).

us also believe in the possibility of enlisting for Christ men and women no longer young.

6. SHOWING THE CONTRASTS OF THE HEREAFTER

Again we turn to our Lord's method of contrast between the good and the evil. In the twenty-fifth chapter we come to perhaps the most difficult and the most important parables in Matthew. In a realm where the most saintly scholars do not always agree, let us not seem dogmatic. Who can feel sure that he has written or spoken the last word about the final return of our Lord? Still we should not pass by the three parables that the evangelist has put just before his account of the Cross. Humbly let us try to translate figure into fact, and then discuss the fact in the light of the figure. Let us seek the heavenly meaning that shines out through the earthly forms. First we shall take up Matt. 25:1-13. For the sake of variety, and symmetry, the plan departs from the twofold structure of the parable.

WAITING FOR THE FINAL RETURN OF OUR LORD

Our Lord teaches much about His final return.
Here He speaks in terms of a wedding feast.
I. The ten maidens represent His professed followers.
   A. "Ten" is a round number with no special significance.
   B. Note the same place—time—posture—purpose.
II. The wise maidens represent His real friends.
   A. When the calls comes, they are prepared.
   B. With Him they enter into the house of gladness.
III. The unwise maidens represent His nominal friends.
   A. They do not care enough to make ready.
   B. They discover their error too late.

The resulting sermon would raise more questions than it answered, but no harm can come from lay thought and prayer about this New Testament teaching. Just now we ought to ask why all ten maidens were not admitted. Why did not the ones who were "ready" share their oil with those who were unprepared? According to Ralph Waldo Emerson and others, they should have done so. But how? Spiritual preparedness here seems to mean Christlike character, as the gift of God in response to faith. If anyone prefers another wording, it means the indwelling of the Holy Spirit. No one can share this kind of "oil." From a different point of view, think about what a scholar of yesterday wrote concerning the type of character that our Lord approved in His sermon-stories:

Modern painters have often pictured Jesus as something of a dreamer, a longhaired, sleepy, abstract kind of person. What a contrast we find in the energy of the real Jesus—in the straight and powerful language which he uses to men. . . . How many of the parables turn on energy? The real trouble with men, he seems to say, is . . . sheer slackness; they will not put their minds to the thing before them, whether it be thought or action. . . . Indecision is one of the things that . . . will keep a man outside the Kingdom of God, . . . unfit for it. . . .
He is always against the life of drift, the half-thought-out life.[9]

On the other hand, the parable gives little encouragement to those who think of the final return in terms of excitement and hysteria on the part of the saints. While awaiting His coming, at a time of which they could not know, the maidens "all slumbered and slept." The wise ones knew that the Lord wished them to sleep. They showed a picture of poise and self-control. When the watchers announced the approach of the bridegroom, the wise maidens arose and trimmed their lamps. All of these details belong in the realm of figure rather than

[9] See T. R. Glover, *The Jesus of History* (New York: Association Press, 1917), pp. 129-31.

fact. Still the figures suggest feelings of joy and hope, kept within bounds, rather than extravagant emotion and ecstatic contortions. "Let your moderation be known unto all men. The Lord is at hand" (Phil. 4:5, K.J.V.) .

In the history of New England, May 19, 1780, has become known for its supposed foreshadowing of the Judgment Day. At noon the skies were turned from blue to gray, and by midafternoon they had become so black that men fell on their knees and cried out to God for mercy ere they went to their doom. On that day the Connecticut House of Representatives was in session. When darkness fell by day, some began to shout and plead for mercy. Others demanded an immediate adjournment. The Speaker of the House, Colonel Davenport, called for silence. Then he spoke: "The Day of Judgment is either approaching or it is not. If it is not, there is no cause for adjournment. If it is, I choose to be found doing my duty. I wish, therefore, that candles be brought." [10]

7. DEALING WITH TIME AND ETERNITY

Again our Lord employs contrast, this time with the stress on the present and the future. In our golden chapter the second parable also has to do with the last things. Here the Master speaks about opportunity, and in terms of investment (Matt. 25:14-30) . The preceding story-sermon moves in a realm that appeals most to women; this one has to do with the workaday world of men. It tells of religion and life, here and hereafter, in terms of investment and returns. Following the structure of the parable itself, we shall look first at what it tells about life here and now, in terms of opportunity. Then we shall see what it shows about life hereafter, with its rewards.

[10] See Alistair Cooke, *One Man's America* (New York: Alfred A. Knopf, 1952) , p. 17.

RELIGION IN TERMS OF INVESTMENT

Among all the parables of Jesus, almost half relate to money. Money here serves as a symbol for opportunity.

I. The Lord as the Giver of opportunity. A talent here means a fortune.

    A. The five-talent man has an exceptional opportunity. Think of Moses or Paul, John Wesley or Albert Schweitzer.

    B. The two-talent man has a large opportunity. Think of Andrew or Thomas—"average men" at work for God.

    C. The one-talent man has a real opportunity. A talent was $1,000 (Goodspeed), perhaps $3,000 today.

       He pities himself and does nothing for God.

II. The Lord as the Rewarder of faithful work

    A. He gives the five-talent man twice as much as before.

       He enables him to become a ten-talent man.

    B. He gives the two-talent man all he can do. Think of Mary Slessor in Calabar.

    C. He gives the one-talent man nothing but a rebuke.

       He was rebuked not because of his poverty, but his attitude.

       He was wicked towards God, and slothful in his work.

The parable keeps the hearer's eye fixed on the persons in this Bible drama. First of all, in the sermon as in the parable, stands the Divine Investor. Both in giving opportunities and in bestowing rewards He dominates the entire action. So He ought to do in the sermon. Before Him, one after another, pass three men, to each of whom He gives as large an opportunity as the man's ability enables him to meet. Later the same men pass before Him again, and in the same order. In personality, both divine and human, and in action, like that of men today, the parable interprets religion by use of money. Our Lord so teaches because He wishes every hearer to dedicate to God all his ability, and then to make the most of every opportunity. For this kind of man, and for him alone, the facts about the unknown future need to bring no dread alarms.

8. PREACHING ABOUT THIS WORLD AND THE NEXT

Once more, our Lord contrasts the world here and now with what lies beyond our ken. The last of the parables in Matthew seems the most difficult of all (25:31-46). It has to do with the final Judgment, on the basis of character and life here and now. In the parable as a whole, and in every part, the Lord Christ Himself stands out as the central Figure, but He does not appear alone. Before Him pass "all the nations." The difficulty in making the parable clear arises partly from the fact that it tells about sheep and goats, whereas the hearers may know little about sheep and nothing about goats.

One interpreter helped to make the idea clear by telling about a scene on a farm in Scotland when he was a boy. Yonder in the meadow half a mile away the farmer has a flock of sheep and a drove of swine, all of them white. Hour after hour they graze together, and only a stockman can tell Merino sheep from Chester White hogs. In the evening they come out of the pasture and find their way to places where they will spend the night. The sheep come into their fold, and the swine go to their sty. The farmer does not "send" them; they go.

Obviously, no one figure can tell the whole truth about such a bewildering reality as the final Judgment. The present sermon-story brings to light one of the basic truths about the Judgment—the separation between the sheep and the nonsheep.

Another way of dealing with the parable would call for a different figure. Almost everyone today knows about some professional school and the regular final examinations. In a certain congregation a young man, widely beloved, has come to the end of his studies in medicine. Shortly he will go before the State Board and take his final comprehensives. If he passes, he will have a right to practice his chosen profession. If not, then not. In order to meet the final comprehensives he has spent ten years in study. After he passes with credit, he will go out into a larger and fuller life. Here again the figure does not convey or suggest all the facts.

Many of us believe that an interpreter has a right to translate a parable from our Lord into thought forms of people today who do not feel at home among sheep and goats. In Alaska a missionary may refer to reindeer rather than sheep. We also feel that the expositor has a right, humbly and reverently, to depart from the structure of the parable so as to teach the same truths in a fashion largely his own. He may seldom feel the necessity of departing from the original framework, but when he does so, he should not apologize. "Where the Spirit of the Lord is, there is freedom" (II Cor. 3:17b). On the other hand, only an experienced interpreter would consider such an undertaking as the one below:

THE JUDGMENT AS OUR FINAL EXAMINATION

I. The Lord Himself will be in charge. Who else has the Character—Wisdom—Authority?

II. He will divide men into two groups. How, we do not know.
   A. He will pass everyone worthy to dwell with God.
   B. He will not pass anyone unfit for heaven.

III. He will judge largely on the basis of kindness. Other factors do not appear in the parable.
   A. He will judge kindness, as to Christ Himself.
   B. He will judge unkindness, as to Christ Himself.

IV. His decisions will fill many with amazement. Not about others, but about ourselves.
   A. Many will be amazed that they have stood the test.
   B. Others will be amazed that they have failed.

This kind of message is expository in substance rather than form, and in spirit rather than structure. Even so, a glance over the sermon plan above will show that every idea has come out of the passage. An expository sermon means the interpretation of life today, in light that comes from God today, largely through a certain portion of Holy Writ. Other aspects of the final judgment appear in other passages, such as II Cor. 5:10, in its context. A systematic theologian would strive to make a synthesis of all these truths. A popular expositor attempts to bring out the truth that the Master Teacher put into a single passage, and in a form that appeals to the imagination.

In the present chapter the examples all point in the same direction. They show that popular exposition of the parables calls for sturdy structure, more or less like that of the parables themselves. If I may paraphrase a saying from our Lord, "Without structure He spake never a parable." In this discussion the stress has fallen even more on the need for varieties in design. At the cost of seeming repetitious let me insist that this kind of pulpit work often suffers from the sort of insipid sameness that Spurgeon characterized as "monotonus regularity." In the Pastor's School he used to say about sermon outlines from his students, "All of them skeletons, without the Holy Spirit." Again he declared, "The surest way to maintain variety is to keep to the mind of the Holy Spirit in the particular passage." [11]

9. LEADING UP TO A CLIMAX

The discussion so far may seem to have ignored or minimized the importance of climax. If so, let me remedy the defect. Thoughtful laymen rightly feel that hearing a sermon ought to seem like a trip through a land of hills and valleys, and that the trail ought to lead upward. Then there will be a few memorable vistas, each of them nobler than the last. In bald prose, arrange for more than one climactic stage in every expository sermon, and be sure that each stage has more intensity of feeling than the one before. All of this is easier to say than to do.

[11] See his wise little book *Lectures to My Students,* first series (London, 1875) , p. 75.

Because of failure to seek and secure climatic moments, an expository sermon may fail to move the hearer Godward.

As a rule the obvious way to secure climax is to follow the general order of the ideas in the passage. Surely one cannot "improve" the order of sacred words. "Oh," says a young man who essays to preach about the two houses, "I must begin with the one on the sand, so as to have a climax. Then I can close with something positive." As for the two houses, which one interests the hearer more? Which one finds its way into the newspapers? In our city this year thousands of structures have risen toward completion. The only one that has appeared on the front page of the morning paper has been one that collapsed. "It fell; and great was the fall of it." As for ending positively, Amen, but do that in a brief conclusion. Base it on the parable as a whole. Strange as the fact may seem, the climax of a sermon usually comes a little while before the conclusion.

Present-day preachers excel in the art of introduction far more than in that of conclusion. If anyone wishes to learn how to start a sermon with absorbing human interest, let him study sermons by pulpit masters of today. If he wishes to build up toward a climax, and then appeal for a verdict, he will do better to go back to foremost preachers of yesterday. These men had the habit of putting near the forefront of a sermon the basic truth, and then building up toward the climax. The climax has far more to do with psychology than with doctrine. In the mind of the preacher, doctrinally, the house on the rock stands first, but in the feelings of the hearer, psychologically, the climax comes with the swish of the waters, the roar of the wind, and the collapse of the house.

Take another concrete example of contrast and climax. On a hot Sunday morning in August a minister preached about the Transfiguration (Matt. 17:1-8, 14-21). As an aid in calling attention to this portion of the gospel he secured from the city library copies of Raphael's masterpiece, *The Transfiguration*. One copy he showed from the pulpit. The others he put on a table and asked the people to examine them at the end of the hour. Of course he began with a text, which he paraphrased, "Master, it is well that we are here; let us stay" (17:4a). Then he announced a subject, "The Gospel According to Raphael." This he followed by holding up the picture, so that everyone could see at least the outline, while he read from the reverse side what the librarians had put there in the way of "adult education":

Raphael's masterpiece, *The Transfiguration,* was painted in 1520. It now hangs in the Vatican Gallery at Rome. This wonderful picture represents two scenes.

At the foot the crowd of people have brought to nine of the disciples a boy possessed with an evil spirit. The demoniac is writhing with anguish, in the arms of his father, who implores the aid of the disciples, but all in vain.

The upper part of the picture shows the glory of Christ. The serene and majestic expression of His face is the greatest charm of the entire painting.

Why did the writer of the sketch begin with the scene at the foot of the mountain? No doubt for the sake of securing climax. The sacred writer knew better. He began with the Lord Christ, who alone made possible the scene down in the valley. Raphael, too, employed all of his art in calling attention first to the Lord of Glory. The painter never would have dreamed of entitling his masterpiece "The Plight of the Demoniac Lad." In order to bring out the primacy of the Redeemer, Raphael showed the lad with eyes lifted up toward the Lord. All the other lines in the picture tend to converge on the One in His glory. In the noblest art of Florence and Rome, whenever our Lord appears in a picture, the light shines fullest and brightest upon His face. What then does the Transfiguration mean for us today? Let us think about it in terms of public worship.

I. The mountaintop shows the spirit of our worship.
   A. We behold the glory of the Redeemer.
   B. We adore Him in a place of beauty.
   C. We see Him with men of the Bible.
   D. We feel a sense of uplift. "It is well [to be] here," but not to stay.
II. The valley shows the meaning of our service.
   A. We behold a case of human need.
   B. We see good men powerless to help.
   C. We watch the healing work of Christ.
   D. We learn the meaning of Christian service.

> O Master, from the mountain side,
>   Make haste to heal these hearts of pain;
> Among these restless throngs abide,
>   O tread the city's streets again.[12]

In this plan, as in the gospel record and in the painting by Raphael, the important part comes first. The climax belongs with what comes toward the end. The spirit that surrounds the Lord with glory on the mountaintop leads to the healing of the lad down in the valley. Here once again, the idea of climax is psychological rather than doctrinal. For confirmation read a textbook that many young people study in college and university, *Practical Psychology* by Dr. F. K. Berrien, of Colgate University. His closing chapter deals with "Effective

---

[12] From the hymn, "Where Cross the Crowded Ways of Life" (1903), by Frank Mason North.

Speaking and Writing." Here he insists on the practical wisdom of "driving to the point" as soon as possible:

Every bit of speaking that must gain attention on its merits should drive immediately to the point. Each opening ought not only to arouse interest but also give more than a broad hint of the essential content of the discourse. The theme is established either in the opening sentence or in the first paragraph.

The importance of driving to the point early in one's presentation was revealed in a study of the memory value of several different kinds of emphasis available to the public speaker. The investigator prepared a short biography which he presented to ten different groups of college students, each time in a different way. The results showed that statements made at the beginning were remembered 75 per cent better than those in the middle of the speech.

The significance of this fact for the public speaker is obvious. If he is sure of the good will of the audience, he can safely present the salient feature of his address at the start, with very good reason to expect that it will impress his listeners. It is certainly true, also, of good speaking that the opening lines must not only compel attention, but must in addition provide a peg on which the subsequent story is hung.[13]

In other words, not psychological, when you preach about the two contrasting scenes at the Transfiguration, begin with the one about the glory of Christ. In dealing with the key verse of the First Gospel, the same principle holds good. "Seek ye first the kingdom of God, and his righteousness; and all these things shall be added unto you" (Matt. 6:33 K.J.V.). The main truth here relates to the kingdom of God, which first of all is divine. The more interesting truth has to do with the by-products of the kingdom. Doctrinally a man would base everything on the doing of God's will. Psychologically he would

[13] P. 513. Copyright 1944 by The Macmillan Co., and used by their permission.

find the people much more concerned about the promise relating to the by-products. The climax would come in showing how the doing of God's will brings freedom from worry about things to eat and wear, to own and enjoy. In preaching about Christ, as in living for Him, put the first thing first.[14]

---

[14] For a fuller discussion of the entire subject, see my *Preparation of Sermons*, Chaps. XI, "The Concern About Structure," XII, "The Variety of Sermon Plans."

CHAPTER SEVEN

THE CONCERN ABOUT A FITTING STYLE

STYLE HERE MEANS THE GARMENT OF WORDS WITH WHICH one clothes the body of truth that enters into a sermon. The term style has nothing to do with seeming stylish. The best sort of writing or speaking about the Lord calls no attention to itself. According to James Denney, "No man can bear witness to Christ and to himself at the same time." [1] This warning works two ways. It discourages "fine writing," which Horace Bushnell would term "the mind's millinery." The idea of calling no attention to the way one speaks also discourages muddiness and ugliness, awkwardness and uncouthness, or anything else out of keeping with the spirit and form of a Bible passage.

Style [is a] curiously personal thing. . . . Literature is not an abstract science, to which exact definitions can be applied. It is an art rather, the success of which depends on personal persuasiveness. . . . Style consists in thinking with the heart as well as with the head. . . . Style . . . is the power to touch with ease, grace, precision, any note in the gamut of human thought or emotion. . . .

[Style] resembles good manners. It comes of endeavoring to understand others, of thinking for them rather than for yourself.[2]

Scholarly expositors, such as John Calvin and George Adam Smith, have excelled in the use of literary style as a means to

---

[1] See *Studies in Theology* (London: Hodder & Stoughton, 1895), p. 161, a priceless book.

[2] Sir Arthur T. Quiller-Couch, *On the Art of Writing* (New York: G. P. Putnam's Sons, 1916), pp. 17, 20, 291, 297.

an end far higher than itself. Various others, later in time, have stressed scholarly exposition, but they have paid small attention to literary form. Hence much of their expository work has lacked clarity and interest, beauty and force. If the message comes from a parable in Luke, for instance, why should the form of the sermon misrepresent the spirit of the passage? However worthy his intentions, a man may serve as a mis-interpreter.

Herein lies much of the difficulty, as well as the fascination, of expository work. The literary form of the sermon ought to accord with the spirit of the parable. Why? Because part of the value in a parable comes from the perfection of its form. Exquisite as a cameo, both as a whole and in every part, a parable shows the magic power of words. However far the interpreter may fall short of his ideal, at least he can strive to clothe every expository message with a fitting garb. In as far as he does so, from parable to parable, he will show variety of literary form, since no two of our Lord's sermon-stories have the same kind of "tone color." From this point of view let us look at parables from Luke. What do the hearers have a right to expect from the expositor in the way of literary style? First of all, they wish to understand him.[3]

1. SEEKING AFTER CRYSTAL CLARITY

Let us begin with the words (Luke 10:25-28) that lead up to the parable about being a good neighbor. In these prelimi-nary verses the dialogue shows "The Meaning of a Man's Religion." Really the expert in Jewish law asked about eternal life, but in terms of today his question has to do with what it means to be a child of God. The two Old Testament sayings

[3] See Rudolf Flesch, *The Art of Plain Talk* (New York: Harper & Bros., 1946).

that our Lord endorsed (Deut. 6:4-5; Lev. 19:18) center round the word "love." Love of this kind leads into a life of service, and even of sacrifice. More important by far, a man's religion consists in loving relations with God. Thus the love concerns three persons. In this working description of a man's religion, note what comes first.

    I. A man's religion consists in loving God supremely.
    II. It includes loving his neighbor largely.
    III. It calls for loving oneself last.

In making ready to preach from this "form of sound words," a man ought to study with care the meaning of the word love, beginning preferably with the Hebrew and the Greek. The Greek term here (*agapao*) rightly looms large in the biblical and theological thinking of our day.[4] This term nobly describes God's feeling toward us, as in John 3:16, and our response to Him, as in I John 4:19, "We love, because he first loved us." According to a useful book of reference, in both hemispheres of the Bible love of this kind means "the response of a man in the totality of his being to the prior love of God. The whole man is the object of the divine love, and the whole man is claimed by God for Himself. The command forces [a] man to a radical decision."[5]

The interpreter ought also to decide what it means for a man to love God with all his heart and soul, strength and mind.

---

[4] See Anders T. Nygren, *Agape and Eros,* 2 parts (New York: The Macmillan Co., 1932, 1939); Nels F. S. Ferré, *The Christian Understanding of God* (New York: Harper & Bros., 1951).

[5] See Alan Richardson, ed., *A Theological Word Book of the Bible* (London: Student Christian Movement Press, 1950), p. 134; also pp. 132-36. Cf. D. W. Eichrodt, *Theologie des Alten Testaments,* 3 vols. (Berlin, 1948), I, chapter on "Die Liebe Gottes."

Surely neither Testament teaches or suggests that a man's inner being, psychologically, consists of a spiritual motor with four cylinders. In speaking to common people the Bible here means that a man ought to love God with all of his redeemed powers. More poetically the psalmist sings, "Bless the Lord, O my soul; and all that is within me, bless his holy name!" (Ps. 103:1.)

Again, the Lord speaks popularly rather than scientifically when He endorses the saying about loving one's neighbor as oneself. Whether or not he should do so, the man in the pew esteems himself highly. This latter part of the Bible passage means much the same as the Golden Rule, "Whatever you wish that men would do to you, do so to them" (Matt. 7:12). In each case the standard has to do with a man's attitude toward himself, as well as others.

By inference our Lord here teaches a man's duty to himself. Not first, or even second, but last of all, he ought to care for himself. He should make the most of his personality, for the sake of his God and the sake of his neighbor. The value of a man's love to God and to others depends much on what he makes of himself. Herein lies the basis of one's concern about education and various other forms of self-improvement. "For their sake I consecrate myself" (John 17:19a). To the contrary, the drunkard does not care for himself enough to keep sober, and the harlot, enough to keep herself pure. So let us never lead young people to sing:

> Oh, to be nothing, nothing,
>   Only to lie at His feet,
> A broken and emptied vessel,
>   For the Master's use made meet.[6]

[6] A gospel song by Georgiana M. Taylor (1869).

If any reader wishes to test the matter of clarity, let him turn to half a dozen scholarly commentaries on the Third Gospel and see if he understands what each of them says about Luke 10:25-28. On the other hand, university professors of English teach that "exposition consists in the simplifying of experience." This our Lord did with the lawyer. Before the conversation ended, the inquirer had learned what he wished to know in answer to an intelligent question. As for ability to live according to this light, such power appears in chapters near the end of Luke. The questioner needed only to trust in the One who on the Cross and at the Resurrection would give the supreme revelation of power for a man's religion.

2. APPEALING TO HUMAN INTEREST

In the parable about the Good Samaritan (Luke 10:30-37), and in every other sermon-story, the quality of interest bulks larger than that of clarity. Not every parable is clear throughout, but every one has untold interest. In the preceding conversation the lawyer seized upon the word "neighbor." Why? Because it interested him most. Then our Lord told him the sermon-story about being a good neighbor. Why? Because of human interest. In terms of today, Christ employed a problem approach, preached a life-situation sermon, offered a moving illustration, or taught by the case method. Whatever the homiletical label, He appealed to the immediate interests of the hearer. By appealing to these interests He conveyed a needed truth. "No man ever spoke like this man!" (John 7:46.)

THE RELIGION OF BEING A GOOD NEIGHBOR

One of the most important questions today
The answer from the Jericho road, the "bloody way"
I. The need of a neighbor's help—the victim of robbers—enemies of mankind—worse than wild beasts

126

II. The lack of a neighbor's heart—professionalism, indifference
   A. The priest's business—to sympathize and help
   B. The Levite's business—to assist the priest
III. The spirit of a neighbor's service—the good Samaritan, a social outcast
   A. Sympathy—putting self in the other man's place
   B. First aid—ministering to his present needs
   C. Self-denial—giving time, strength, money
   Not, "Who is my neighbor?" but "Whose neighbor am I?"

How can the interpreter secure like interest? In preaching to university students about this parable former Dean Charles R. Brown of Yale stressed three things: "What is yours is mine." "What is mine is my own." "What is mine is yours." Note the simplicity and the human interest. Behold three sorts of men. Who else in three short sentences could have summed up the teaching of the parable? In the sermon that centered around these headings the dean showed that the whole matter had to do with the young man in the pew. Like the Master Himself, Dean Brown stressed one man at a time, and always with interest.

Another university divine dealt with the parable impersonally. In a chapter about "The Teaching of Jesus Concerning the Care of the Poor" this professor of Christian morals used the parable as an example of what experts in social welfare strive to accomplish for people in distress. A comparison between the personal terms of the parable and the abstractions that now follow will show much, positively and negatively, about the secret of appealing to human interest.

Nothing can describe with more precision the exact programme which scientific charity has by degrees worked out to guide the visitation of the poor—first, friendly compassion, . . . then the transfer of the case to restorative conditions, finally the use of money, not as alms for the helpless, but to maintain continuity of relief. . . .

The reform in method now proposed in the name of scientific charity is, in reality, nothing else than a return to the principles of the Good Samaritan.

Two words sum up the change of method advocated at the present time. . . . The first word is classification; the second is anti-institutionalism.[7]

Unlike this excerpt the parable has to do only with facts about persons. Except for the robbers, who quickly fade from view, the persons appear one by one, and in contrast. The types stand out boldly. They also reveal character by action. Out of 150 words in the main part of the sermon-story, a certain student has found 27 verbs full of action. These words convey a sense of conflict and struggle, suspense and progress, with at last a solution. This abstract statement of facts can never do justice to the way the Master Artist uses words to interpret an important aspect of life. If anyone would learn how to excel in "the art of being interesting," let him study this parable, first as a whole and later word by word. Then he will keep away from such jargon as "classification" and "anti-institutionalism."

3. USING ALL SORTS OF FACTS

The use of concrete facts relates to human interest, as above, but the matter deserves attention by itself. In large measure the popular preachers of our day have learned the wisdom of employing facts, but not every would-be expositor has mastered this part of his lifework. As with other ways of securing interest, he can do no better than study the parables, one by one. Just now he may deal with "The Pagan Philosophy of a Rich Fool." One of us might hesitate to call a rich farmer a fool, because we adopt his way of looking at life. Fortunately, we have a word

[7] See Francis G. Peabody, *Jesus Christ and the Social Question* (New York: The Macmillan Co., 1900), pp. 250-51. The passage also shows lack of rhythm.

painting from the Master Artist. As often elsewhere, He uses money to interpret religion (Luke 12:13-21).

I. The philosophy of a rich fool (vss. 16-19). Every man has a working philosophy of life.
   A. The philosophy of an egotist—living for self. He uses 61 words—13 references to self; none to others.
   B. The philosophy of a materialist—living for things. His creed is "Things!"—not bad things, but things.
   C. The philosophy of an atheist—not living for God. He makes no reference to God's gifts, rights, claims.
II. The folly of this philosophy (vss. 20-21)
   A. The folly of not living for others—a loss of usefulness[8]
   B. The folly of not living to give—a loss of happiness
   C. The folly of not living for God—a loss of blessedness

After this quick survey the facts may seem prosaic. If so, they need to assume other forms. In the parable the facts stand out true to life. They all relate to a rich farmer, like a man in Nebraska or Illinois today. With few changes in phrasing the same word picture would hold true of a merchant or a banker in town. The practical philosophy here resembles that of a man today who gets rich, and in so doing runs the risk of losing his soul. But why state the facts abstractly? The parable shows them in terms of storing grain, pulling down barns, and building larger ones, so as to care for increased crops.

In looking at a rich farmer any city man can see the folly of living for things, for self, for here and now, so as ignore and lose "the things that money cannot buy." The pastor's shelves contain various classic works, such as Goethe's *Faust* and Dickens' *Christmas Carol*, which make clear the folly of

[8] See James M. Barrie, *The Twelve Pound Look*, in *Representative Plays*, ed. by Wm. L. Phelps (New York: Chas. Scribner's Sons, 1918).

shortsightedness in a man who does not live on a farm. Any minister who would lead such a hearer into the Christian way of living must know how to present his case in fact forms of our day. Where in the Bible can anyone find a better case than in this parable?

Every summer for more than two score years the late George W. Truett of Dallas traveled seven hundred miles out to West Texas and preached to cattlemen, including owners of ranches and bands of cowboys. Often he spoke about what we call stewardship, better known as trusteeship. After one service a ranchman took the preacher for a walk. Apart from other men the cattleman asked the minister to offer a prayer of dedication.

I have not been a Christian long, and I do not know much about the Christian life. I have learned today, as never before, what the Christian life means. Now I see that every hoof of all these thousands of cattle belongs to Christ, and that every acre over which they range belongs to Christ. . . . I want you to tell God for me that I will be His trustee from this day on. . . . When you finish telling Him that for me, you wait. I have got something to tell Him myself.[9]

The minister dedicated to the Lord all of that man's worldly goods. Then the ranchman, with tears streaming down his face, prayed to God for the conversion of his wayward son:

I have given you my property today, and I will from now on be your administrator on your estate. And now, won't you take my boy in the same way, and save him, and save him soon, for your glory?

That night the son gave himself to the Saviour. This experience shows the spirit in which the interpreter ought to deal with such a portion of God's Book, and with such a man of wealth. "I seek not what is yours but you" (II Cor. 12:14b) .

[9] See Powhatan W. James, *George W. Truett: A Biography* (Rev. ed.; New York: The Macmillan Co., 1945) , pp. 112-13.

Preach much about money. Be sure to show how it may become a means of grace, not a millstone around the neck.

4. CULTIVATING A SENSE OF BEAUTY

In order to interpret any parable or psalm a minister needs a sense of beauty. Like Bishop William A. Quayle one should be able to qualify as a "poet-preacher." Nowhere in the Bible can a lover of quiet beauty find more of it than in the fifteenth chapter of Luke. Since the tone color of an expository sermon ought to accord with that of the passage in hand, how can anyone dare to preach from this chapter? At least one can make the attempt. Even while conscious of falling short one can cherish the ideal. As Robert Browning says,

> Ah, but a man's reach should exceed his grasp,
> Or what's a heaven for?

If a man lives with the Master's words, full of simple beauty, and preaches from them at times, he will become like what he loves.

A British divine has a sermon about the chapter as a whole, under the heading "Christ Concerning the Lost." Except for a pastor and a people who have become accustomed to expository preaching, a sermon about finding the lost sheep, the lost coin, and the lost boy would contain too much material. What can a man omit? On the other hand, the three parables belong together, as three companion pictures with the same motif. This fact the British preacher brings out in his brief words of introduction. Since he plans to deal with all three parables, he wastes no time in getting started. The entire introduction appears below. It grows out of the text, "He told them this parable" (15:3) .

"This parable," not these parables. The window is one, though it has three panes. The clover is one, though it bears three leaves. God is one, though manifested in three Persons. The parable is one, though divided into three parts.

From this great utterance of our Lord we learn His thought and feeling concerning that which is lost.[10]

The last and best (15:11-32) of these three sermon-stories centers around the father, but the hearer may expect a message about the younger son. Really we know little about his age, but we may think of him as twenty-one. Also we may speak of the far country in terms of a large city today. That is where a young man seeks an outlet for his pent-up energies. Really we know next to nothing about what the prodigal did there with his father's money. We have no evidence except that of the elder brother, who spoke out of spite. Still we know much about this kind of young fellow today. He feels that he must turn his back on the old farm home and seek a freer life in the purlieus of a city. He may be mistaken about both farm and city. The fact remains that the farmer's son or daughter may yield to the attractions of the vast unknown, only to find in it disappointment, ruin, and shame.

A Present-Day Version of the Supreme Parable

I. The temptations of the young man on the farm relate to work
—play—companions—money

II. The wrongdoings of the young man far from home
A. Wasting his substance
B. Living for himself
C. Causing injury to others
D. Forgetting about God

III. The awakening of the young man in distress
A. Coming to himself and feeling sorry

[10] See J. D. Freeman, *Concerning the Christ* (Cincinnati: Jennings and Main, n.d.), pp. 173-90. A full outline appears in my *Preaching from the Bible*, pp. 144-45.

    B. Confessing all his sins
    C. Starting back to his father's house
IV. The welcome for the young man back at home
    A. Welcome for a beloved son
    B. Forgiveness for all the past
    C. Joys in the father's home

The sermon a week later may deal with "A Present-Day Picture of the Elder Brother." His temptations and sins appear almost the reverse of those relating to his younger brother. The elder brother's temptations were too much work, too little play, too few companions, and too much concern about hoarding money. His sins were ingratitude to his father, intolerance to his brother, and pride in himself. In the eyes of our Lord these sins are worse than the more spectacular transgressions of the younger son. Because of Pharisees and scribes who resembled the elder brother, and sneered at the Lord's kindness to men like the prodigal, the Master Teacher spoke the three companion parables. The reason appears in 15:1-3.

It requires much more courage and skill to preach about the elder brother than about the younger one. After a minister had explained what the parable suggests about the sins of a farmer in middle age, a lay officer of this sort spoke out indignantly, "Your sermon runs counter to all that my dear old father taught me." Evidently the middle-aged critic thought about the importance of staying at home, working hard, and saving money. The sermon must have missed its mark in dealing with sin, for no worthy father ever taught his son to admire ingratitude, intolerance, and insufferable egotism. As F. W. Robertson used to insist, it is harder to bring to repentance a worldly man who lives for money than a social outcast ashamed of his sins.

I once knew a farmer of middle age who bore a name resembling that of "Mr. Neighbor." He had all the strong points of the elder brother, and all the weaknesses. This farmer worked hard, made money, and kept it. The more he made the more he wanted to make. He had no friends, and he desired none. He prided himself on indifference to God, superiority to more easygoing neighbors, and success in making money. At last his nerves gave way, and he could toil no more. Then he began to rail at neighbors who ignored him as he had ignored them. "Whatever a man sows, that he will also reap" (Gal. 6:7c). I used to visit this self-centered farmer, both before his loss of health and afterward, but I never succeeded in getting him to see anything lacking in himself, or anything right with anyone else, even with God.

Once again, the pastor ought to preach about "The Gospel of the Loving Father." In the twenty-two verses of the parable the word father rings out twelve times. The story-sermon leads us to look on God as Father, and as Lover of both sons. Think of His love for a young man like the prodigal, a love that never will let him go, a love that draws him safely home. Then behold the love of God for an older son who never has dreamed that he is a sinner. If the parable tells nothing about what God the Father has done for the prodigal and his brother, through Christ and the Cross, this part of the Gospel appears a little later in Luke. In its fullness and power the old, old story has a way of reaching even a middle-aged sinner whose heart has grown hard through lack of love. Still it is easier to win the younger man. He too needs the Heavenly Father.

The spirit of the parable came out in an experience of a well-known pastor in New York City. Once a week he called on a young physician who was wasting away because of misspent physical powers. At each visit the minister read from the Bible and offered a brief prayer. One day, unintentionally, he left his New Testament at home. So he repeated from memory, word for word, the parable of the Loving Father. At the end of

134

the recital the pastor said to the young man, whom he had known from boyhood, "John, why did that young fellow come back home?"

"He must have got tired of living on husks."

"No, John, you have long been tired of husks."

"Tell me the story again, please." The minister did so. "I see it now! He found that he loved his father." Then John gave his heart to God.

In this fifteenth chapter the three sermon-stories belong to what Thomas De Quincey calls "the literature of feeling" rather than "the literature of thought." All of them, especially the third, show that when a speaker's heart is moved, his words flow with a pleasing rhythm. In preaching about any aspect of the threefold parable one ought to use words full of quiet beauty. In order to do so one ought to live with these forms of beauty day after day until one's heart begins to glow. Then one can share with lay friends the wonders of redeeming love.

From a different point of view, the last few paragraphs remind us that the form of an expository sermon need not follow the order of ideas in the passage. By singling out at different times the younger son, the elder brother, and the father of them both, the pastor can deal with characters like the friends in the pew, or like others whom they love. All the biblical facts may come out of the passage. Any one of these sermons ought to bring an interpretation of life today, in light that comes from a certain portion of God's Written Word. In an expository sermon nothing else ought to matter supremely, provided the hearer responds to this new revelation of redeeming love and grace.

5. APPRAISING ONE OF YOUR SERMONS

How should the minister judge his own sermons? He should judge them not so much by clarity, human interest, and quiet beauty as by effectiveness, or force. He may think of those three other qualities as God-given means to this lofty end, force. The term means not clamor that calls attention to itself, but effectiveness in moving the hearer to act. Does the message lead the unsaved hearer to accept the Saviour, and cause the believer in God to love Him better, so as to engage in His service? This quality of force is more difficult to attain than any or all of the others. Let us think of effectiveness in a sermon about a subject as difficult as it is delicate, that of hell.

In His parables, as elsewhere in His recorded teachings, our Lord teaches as much about hell as about heaven, and often in the same connection. According to the Gospels, He utters more on this subject than all of the apostles and prophets combined. Today by His Spirit He is waiting to guide and restrain the humble minister who desires to interpret and illuminate this aspect of revealed truth. Otherwise any man ought to shrink from the task. According to saintly Robert Murray McCheyne, over in Dundee, the minister who preaches about hell ought to do so with tears in his voice. What then can he say about the parable in Luke 16:19-31?

THE CONTRASTS IN THE WORLD TO COME

A word study in black and white. More of shadow than sunshine
  I. The two men here on earth (vss. 19-21)
     A. The rich man without a heart
     B. The poor man without a friend
 II. The two men in the world to come (vss. 22-23)
     A. "The poor man" at a feast
     B. "The rich man" in torment
III. The two sides of the chasm there (vss. 24-26)
     A. The cry from the other side
     B. The lack of a connecting bridge
 IV. The two ways of regarding hell (vss. 27-31)
     A. The concern in the other world
     B. The indifference here on earth

"Many of the words of Jesus are best understood when least explained." The words of this parable tell their own story. They prove most effective when they speak as to a child, and when the interpreter does not attempt to be wise "above that which is written." In the days of His flesh our Lord stressed the reality of both heaven and hell, but he left many of our questions unanswered. Rather did He set up along life's highway certain danger signals. Today He keeps asking, "What are you doing with Lazarus at your door?" In response to the appeal of this parable John Ruskin seems to have changed his ways of living. He had never been a scoundrel, but near the end of his thirty-fifth year he experienced a change of heart. During more than forty years thereafter he strove to serve rather than be served.

My next birthday is the keystone of my life. Up to this time I cannot say that I have in any way "taken up my cross" or denied myself anything. Neither have I visited the poor or fed them, but I have spent my money and my time on my own pleasures and instruction. I cannot be easy in doing this any more, for I feel that if I were to die at present God might justly say to me, "Thou in thy lifetime receivedst thy good things and likewise Lazarus his evil things." I find myself always doing what I like, and that is certainly not the way to heaven.[11]

The effectivenes of the sermon, under God, may depend on the expositor's ability to bring out the contrast between two sorts of men, and then lead the hearer to do now what John Ruskin did at the age of thirty-five. For a more recent example of a changed life because of this parable turn to the autobiog-

[11] See Sir E. T. Cook, *The Life of Ruskin* (New York: The Macmillan Co., 1911), p. 326. For another case see A. J. Cronin, *Adventures in Two Worlds* (New York: McGraw-Hill Book Co., 1952), p. 274. Dr. Cronin saw the light when about thirty-seven years of age.

raphy of Dr. Albert Schweitzer.[12] Throughout the sermon keep the hearer's eye fixed on successive scenes in this moving parable, and on the contrast between the two men directly in view. On the human level focus attention most of all upon Dives, or rather, upon this kind of man today. In other words, take for granted the truthfulness of the word picture. Likewise follow its restraint. Use exposition rather than argument. Let the sermon be dramatic, in the sense of bringing out the action in the parable, rather than dogmatic, in the spirit of "laying down the law." At the end, let us hope, the parable rather than the sermon will bring the hearer to his knees. So let the Lord through the story-sermon speak to the heart of the local Dives today.

6. APPEALING TO THE IMAGINATION

Under God the secret of effectiveness in expository work lies largely in reverent use of imagination. In the hours of study a man looks on a parable as "the gift of God to the imagination." In the pulpit he strives to translate each parable into terms of today. If he succeeds, the hearer sees the truth as it comes from Christ. Then the truth leads him to feel and to act as the Spirit guides. All of this ought to appear in a message about the Pharisee and the tax collector, one of our Lord's most moving sayings about prayer (Luke 18:9-14). Here again the parable embodies the idea of contrast.

TWO MEN AT PRAYER IN PUBLIC

Same place—time—purpose—posture (vs. 10)
Each man much concerned about money
I. A word picture of a snob who prattles (vss. 11-12)

[12] See *Out of My Life and Thought* (New York: Henry Holt & Co., 1933). The suggestion comes from the *Interpreter's Bible* (New York and Nashville: Abingdon-Cokesbury Press, 1952), VIII, 289.

    A. Thanksgiving—all about self
    B. Confession—not a word
    C. Petitions—none at all
II. A word picture of a sinner who prays (vs. 13)
    A. Frankly confesses his sins
    B. Leaves many things unsaid
    C. Casts himself on the mercy of God
Each man gets what he wants, and no more (vs. 14).

On paper this account seems insipid. In the hands of one who uses imagination reverently these simple truths glow with light from God and burn their way into the heart. At the Chapel of Princeton Seminary, Dr. Emil Brunner once preached from this parable. After a few paragraphs of exposition he began dealing with the men in terms of today. Ere long he had the shivers running up and down the spinal column of more than one hearer, whether professor or student. The speaker kept holding up the parable as a mirror before the eyes of the man in the pew, who kept saying to himself, "You are that Pharisee. You ought to be doing what that publican did." No hearer thought of the way the man in the pulpit brought about this effect. Every listener knew that he had come face to face with the Living Christ. What else does it mean to preach? [13]

The man with imagination uses it in sensing the need of the hearers today. In addressing men who tend to substitute religious practices for transforming experiences, he wishes to bring a heartwarming message about the difference between the man who prattles and the one who prays. The preacher does not hesitate to choose a familiar parable, familiar because of its appeal to the eye of the soul. With this sermon-story he lives until his heart begins to burn. Then he stands in the pulpit to

[13] While not always in accord with Dr. Brunner or Dr. Barth, doctrinally, the writer has learned much from both of them, homiletically.

make the other man's heart burn within him as he comes face to face with the Christ who feels much concern about every man's prayers.

Among the assets of a good man called of God to preach expository sermons nothing else bulks larger than imagination. In certain expository sermons, so called, nothing else seems so lacking. As Robert Browning would say, they are "clods, untroubled by a spark." How can a young expositor develop imagination? Mainly by using it. Use it when out among men. What do they most need today, down in their hearts? They need God. Help them find Him in one of the parables, all of which have come through an inspired imagination. Use this God-given power in preparing and preaching a message to set the hearer's soul aflame. In the words of a seaman to old Father Taylor, apostle to the mariners at Boston, "Take something hot out of your heart and thrust it into mine."

After a "sermon" in which the Master Preacher interpreted the Book, His two listeners said to each other, "Did not our hearts burn within us while he talked to us on the road, while he opened to us the scriptures?" (Luke 24:32.) These words near the end of "the most beautful book ever written" remind us that the Third Gospel embodies the sort of preaching style which the present chapter holds up as ideal. If any minister wishes to preach with imaginative power, more and more as the years go by, he can do no better than to saturate his soul in Luke, and in the Psalms. The spirit of the Third Gospel appears in words from a foremost New Testament scholar:

All through the book, we are struck by the note of warm human feeling, in contrast to a certain austerity in Matthew. It is hardly accidental that so many of Luke's scenes are laid at a dinner-table, while Matthew prefers scenes where Jesus is on a mountain-top. We might put it this way: if in Mark Jesus appears as the heroic Leader, and in Matthew as the great Teacher and Law-Giver, in Luke he is above all the Friend of Humanity.[14]

Nowhere in Luke does this warm, intimate quality appear more winsomely than in the sacred record of the walk to Emmaus (24:13-35). This gospel account may lead to a sermon about "The Christian Secret of Radiance." At the opening of the scene two believers in God walk and talk together as though life had lost all its luster, and as though it were no longer worth what it cost. In this mood a man and his wife may come to church today. After an hour or so with the Risen Lord the two pilgrims on the Emmaus road have risen to "the heights of Christian blessedness." On this new and higher level they will live and bear witness until the end of their days on earth. In this passage the evangelist gives an ideal picture of Christian worship. At its best it brings jaded believers a feeling of uplift and power. Today, as on the road to Emmaus, Christian radiance comes through:

I. Being with the Living Christ
II. Understanding the Scriptures
III. Engaging in Christian service
IV. Living in Christian hope

Later that evening the two pilgrims burst into the presence of the apostolic band to tell about the Risen Lord. "They told what had happened on the road, and how he was known to them in the breaking of the bread" (24:35). They had discovered the most exciting good news of history—the resurrection of Christ! Whether Cleopas and his comrade later served

[14] See Charles H. Dodd, *About the Gospels* (Cambridge: University Press, 1950), p. 33.

as full-time ministers we do not know. Of this much we can feel sure: as long as in spirit they lived close to the Risen Lord, and to the Book that made Him known, they showed the meaning of Christian radiance. If any interpreter today fulfills the same conditions, he can experience the same transforming power.

Let us now return to the point where we started the present discussion of literary style. In expository preaching today, as when our Lord opened up the Scriptures, effectiveness depends largely on literary form. This in turn, as Sir Arthur T. Quiller-Couch insists, is not a science to be learned by use of the brain, but an art to be mastered in more elusive ways. In all these holy concerns

> It is the heart, and not the brain,
> That to the highest doth attain.

On the other hand, anyone whom the Lord honors by calling him to become an expository preacher can learn how to speak with clarity and interest, as well as quiet beauty and convincing power, largely by putting to effective use his God-given imagination.[15]

In the literary form of a sermon, as in everything else that a minister does for God, only his best can begin to be good enough to represent the King of Kings. So the man of God ought to shun what Bishop William A. Quayle terms "the sin of being uninteresting." The interpreter ought also to dread the idea of calling attention to himself and away from his Lord. Again the bishop speaks, to show the difference between the

---

[15] For a fuller discussion of sermonic style see my *Preparation of Sermons*, chaps. XV, "The Habit of Writing Sermons," and XVI, "The Marks of Effective Style."

style of the non-Christian orator and that of the Christian interpreter: "Cicero lived for self and self-applause, for self-enrichment and self-service. And Paul lived not for himself, but unto God. Good night, Marcus Tullius Cicero. Ah, Brother Paul! Good morning!" [16]

[16] *The Pastor-Preacher* (New York: Methodist Book Concern, 1910), pp. 124, 299.

CHAPTER EIGHT

THE CALL FOR A PLEASING DELIVERY

O FTEN THE THINGS THAT MATTER MOST LIE AT THE MERCY of those that matter least." Nowhere does this maxim apply more clearly than in expository preaching today. The gospel message with all of its helpfulness and power lies at the mercy of the speaker's voice and manner in the pulpit. On the other hand, the effectiveness of expositors has often been due to their mastery of public speech. In almost every such discourse that I recall with satisfaction the effect came from the delivery more than from anything else. In each case the minister interpreted his passage with eye and hand, as well as voice and word.

The examples now must come from men no longer in the flesh, including some whom I have not heard. These men have also preached in ways not expository, but never more skillfully than when making the hearer see and feel the meaning of a parable or a psalm: Robertson and Maclaren, G. Campbell Morgan and John Henry Jowett, George W. Truett and James Black. Any reader can bring the list down to date, only to find that his expository heroes have differed in many other ways but that all alike have owed much of their effectiveness to mastery of the speaker's art. This aspect of expository preaching has received little attention from writers on the subject, and less attention from would-be expositors. Here follow a number of practical suggestions about "conditioning the desired response." At present this means preparing to speak so as to bring about the result desired.

1. CATCHING THE ATTENTION OF THE HEARER

Under God the effectiveness of a spoken sermon depends on the hearer as much as on the speaker. In an ideal expository situation the hearer brings his Bible to church. Suppose that a pastor has made ready for a number of consecutive sermons from the Book of Acts. He wishes the lay hearers to read this book at home. So he prepares an introductory sermon about "The Most Exciting Book in the New Testament," a topic that comes from Dr. Harris E. Kirk of Baltimore. Without dangling a skeleton before the eyes of his friends, the pastor brings out what he wishes the hearers to see and feel when they read this book at family prayers and at other times. He shows that this exciting book has to do with the super-atomic energy of Almighty God. In our own day, as of old, this almighty power can transform the heart of a person, the life of a community, or the character of a world. On every page of the record God's power to transform appears in a new way. The most exciting book in the New Testament shows the power of God at work:

I. In promoting the Gospel among the Jews (chs. 1-12)
   A. Establishing the Church of Christ (chs. 1-5)
   B. Extending the Church beyond Judea (chs. 6-11)
   C. Transferring the center of work (ch. 12)
II. In promoting the Gospel among the Gentiles (chs. 13-28)
   A. Establishing the Church (13-16:5)
   B. Extending the Church (16:6-19)
   C. Transferring the center (chs. 20-28)[1]

This outline scarcely justifies the topic about the book as exciting. In an introductory sermon the pastor need not stress

[1] Suggested by R. B. Rackham, *The Acts of the Apostles*, "Westminster Commentaries" (London: Methuen & Co., 1902), expensive, but perhaps the best book of its kind.

his outline so much as his purpose. Using some such guide of thought as the above, he can "survey" the book here and there, so that the hearer will determine to read it at home. In like manner at Chautauqua Professor William Lyon Phelps of Yale used to deal with Robert Browning's masterpiece, *The Ring and the Book*. In the opening lecture the genial scholar would show the hearer what the book was about, and then tell only enough to make the listener eager to read it himself. The resulting desire came far more from the contagious enthusiasm of the speaker than from the substance of what he said about the exciting poem. With The Acts of the Holy Spirit, as with *The Ring and the Book,* no man ought to make such an attempt until he senses the power of the work in hand, and feels its excitement.

The most exciting book in the New Testament speaks with special force in days of calamity and chaos. So it has proved helpful of late among Christians in Germany. In a recent year Dr. Martin Dibelius made a speaking tour of our country. At various centers this New Testament scholar told about the plight of his fatherland, but without a touch of bitterness or despair. He pictured Christian homes and churches in ruins, boys and girls facing starvation, and young people with nothing in sight worth living for. He told a gloomy tale, but not with a tragic ending. After a while the learned speaker showed why he and his believing friends in Germany did not feel downcast. "We are living in the Acts of the Apostles, and oh, it is glorious!" In a world that has suffered from two global wars, and lives in dread of still another, most deadly of all, how glorious to trust in the super-atomic power of God!

Somehow get the hearer to share your excitement about this book. Persuade him to read it at home, in the spirit of prayer. Also invite him to bring his New Testament to church.

2. ENCOURAGING THE USE OF THE BIBLE

Many laymen would bring their Bibles to church and keep them open if the pastor made it seem worth while to do so. Why do lovers of classic music take with them to the concert hall their copies of Handel's *Messiah* or Bach's *B Minor Mass*? Because they wish to follow the score. For a similar reason a pastor over in Jersey requests the people to read responsively from their Bibles and not from the church hymnal. He also invites them to follow in their Bibles the reading of the two lessons, one from each Testament. As for the passage that undergirds the sermon, he may use this paragraph as a part of the message proper. On a Lord's Day soon after Easter he wishes to preach about the longing for a revival today. The sermon proper may begin with Acts 2:1-4, a portion of what he has read as the New Testament lesson. Here he follows the principle of repetition for emphasis. After repeating from memory the four verses, he makes a slight pause. Then he quotes the text: "When the day of Pentecost had come, they were all together in one place" (Acts 2:1).

WANTED TODAY: A REVIVAL LIKE PENTECOST

I. It begins with united prayer.
II. It calls for fervent preaching.
III. It comes through personal work.
IV. It leads to widespread repentance.

So the sermon might go on to speak about personal piety and generous giving, but why not stop with repentance? As Robertson used to advise, "Preach suggestively, not exhaustively." Instead of getting the hearer to understand all about Pentecost of old, lead him to pray and work for this kind of renewal here and now. Thus you may dispel some of his doubts about the whole matter of revivals. Instead of arguing with him, or trying to prove a case by logic, point out where in this part of the Acts you find the main truths of the sermon. In a certain sanctuary the pastor occasionally has the people read a verse or two aloud, in concert. "Concert reading from the Bible as a part of public worship?" Why not? "Co-operative preaching" lets the people take part.

This may sound more like teaching an adult Bible class than like an important part of public worship. If so, the fault lies with the description, not with the reality. The practice of bringing the Bible to church and keeping it open during the sermon ought never to interfere with the spirit and the practice of worship. Neither should the custom divert the speaker from his purpose. He aims not merely to explain the passage in view, but to use it in meeting a need today. In dealing with a portion of the Acts he is showing the hearer how to read the book at home and how to pray for the coming of a revival. How long can Protestantism hope to flourish unless our laymen begin again to know and use the Bible?

"Will city men as well as women bring their Bibles to church and keep them open during the service?" The answer must vary according to the courage and the resourcefulness of the leader in the pulpit. For twenty-five years at a large downtown church in Philadelphia throngs of men and women have brought their Bibles and kept them open on the Lord's Day, both morning and evening. They still do so because their pastor still expects them to do so. With Bibles open while he deals with a certain passage in a way all his own, they receive the Word with eagerness of heart. Later at home they examine the Scriptures to see whether these things are so (Acts 17:11).

This man's methods and his message do not appeal to many of his ministerial brethren, some of whom may wonder at this account. They ought to know that the pastor enlists and retains the loyalty of many gifted laymen. He gets them to understand and love the Bible from a point of view distinctly his own. Also, he encourages many of them to teach the Bible elsewhere. All of this he makes possible largely through a dynamic personality, and by emphasis on the use of the open Bible during every sermon.

3. READING THE BIBLE IN WORSHIP

Effectiveness in popular expository work depends in part on ability to read the Holy Scriptures as the most important part of public worship. For instance, the message of the day is to show "The Christian Secret of Courage." "When they saw the boldness of Peter and John, and perceived that they were uneducated, common men, they wondered; and they recognized that they had been with Jesus" (Acts 4:13) . For the New Testament lesson the pastor is to read Acts 3:1-10, about the healing of the lame beggar at the Beautiful Gate of the temple. As the basis of the sermon he is to read the verses surrounding the text, that is, Acts 4:1-22. Under God the effectiveness of the sermon that follows will depend largely on the skill and the care with which the interpreter deals with the Scripture lesson.[2]

When a man wishes people to understand a "lesson," he reads it deliberately. Also he brings out the rhythm. First in the original tongue and then in recent translations of the Bible, he enters into the spirit of the passage and begins to sense its onward flow. He ought to study the best available translations, notably the *Revised Standard Version*.[3] If he wishes the people to follow the reading in public, probably he should use in the pulpit the version that most of them prefer. Whatever the version, he will find that every part of the Holy Writ suitable for public worship has a rhythm all its own. Only at the risk of misrepresenting words full of truth and power dare anyone

[2] On the importance of public Bible reading see James Black, *The Mystery of Preaching* (New York: Fleming H. Revell & Co., 1924) , pp. 234-37.
[3] New York: Thomas Nelson & Sons, 1946, 1952. In public I read the K.J.V.

rush through a holy passage without a pause, and deal with it all regardless of rhythm. "Emphasis is exposition." Now let us glance at the basic framework of the sermon from Acts 4:1-22, with the stress on vs. 13.

I. The Christian meaning of courage
   A. Standing up for Christ in Jerusalem
   B. Speaking out for Him before His slayers
   C. Facing death for Christ and His Church
II. The Christian secret of courage
   A. Being in the School of Christ
   B. Being at the Cross of Christ
   C. Being filled with His Spirit

Before anyone can read the two Bible passages aloud, and then deliver the sermon, he must enter into the spirit of the scene. One way to do that would be to go through Bunyan's little book, *The Jerusalem Sinner Saved*. There the interpreter from Bedford shows that in "beginning at Jerusalem" the apostles needed courage born of God. Did they not know that the "Holy City" had become "the very sink of iniquity and [the] seat of hypocrisy, [the] gulf where religion was drowned"? Could they not look out over Jerusalem as "the very slaughter-house of saints"? Why then did they dare to heal and preach in the name of the One whom the leaders in that city had hounded to His Cross? Because they had been with Jesus. What a succession of overtones ought to accompany the pulpit reading of a passage from the most exciting book in the New Testament! Like the apostles when on trial, however, the reader ought to keep his excitement under control.

4. TREATING THE PEOPLE KINDLY

Both in reading the lessons and in delivering the sermon speak to the people as their friend. Take for granted that they have come to discover the will of God, and with a desire to do it. As for an occasional cantankerous critic who would take delight in watching the "parson" demolish an imaginary man of straw, do not let a cynic's presence interfere with a friendly message to those who have a "will to believe." Think kindly of your hearers. Believe in them. Expect much from them. Show them that you speak as their friend. In the Book of Acts note how kindly Philip dealt with the eunuch, and Peter with the new friends in the house of Cornelius. If a man loves people, and if he loves the Book, he will try to persuade and win, rather than prove and attack. In certain other kinds of pulpit work he may feel obliged to attack occasionally, but in expository preaching he should delight in what Jowett used to term "the wooing note."

For example, the minister knows that some of his leading women will not speak to one another, and that cliques have begun to form within the home church. Also he senses the lack of a forgiving spirit out in the community, and far beyond. Both in the church and throughout the community the pastor loves people who do not like one another. How can he discuss this problem without adding fuel to the flames? By speaking and acting as a Christian gentleman, and as a loving friend. In the spirit of good will, and with tact, though never with compromise of conscience, he can take up a case in his source book. In almost every major part of the Bible he can find some such case, notably in Stephen's dying prayer for those who had done him the deadliest of wrongs. "Lord, do not hold this sin against them" (Acts 7:60b).

THE FORGIVENESS OF DEADLY WRONGS
I. A study in the Christian meaning of forgiveness
   A. The man who endures the wrongs—a saint
   B. The wrongs the saint endures—deadly
   C. The ones who do him wrong—church leaders

D. The only one who can forgive—the victim
II. A study in the Christian spirit of forgiveness
    A. Like that of Christ on the Cross
    B. Leads the innocent one to act
    C. Prays for the wrongdoers
    D. Blesses the onlooker (Saul)

For a living commentary on the Christian meaning of forgiveness turn to one of the best-written novels of our time, *Cry, the Beloved Country*. The book has to do with South Africa, its racial tension, its overcrowding, its underpaid workers, and its other social ills. The action centers round Stephen Kumalo, an aged Negro pastor, and James Jarvis, a wealthy white planter, both of whom live in the same community. In time Jarvis loses a noble son, who is murdered without cause, and Kumalo loses a wayward son, who is hanged, no doubt justly. Apart from the Spirit of Christ either father might blame the other one, but these two men continue to respect and love each other. The spirit of the book, and some of its beauty, appears in the following excerpt, which tells how a native pastor reads from the Bible:

The voice was of gold, and the voice had love for the words it was reading. The voice shook and beat and trembled, not as the voice of an old man shakes and beats and trembles, . . . but as a deep bell when it is struck. For it was not only a voice of gold, but it was the voice of a man whose heart was golden, reading from a book of golden words.[4]

In any hour of crisis a man shows his heart, if he has a heart to show. In reading the Scriptures and in preaching from the Book the late George W. Truett could show that he felt what he was saying. After the most critical week in all his long career

[4] Alan Paton, *Cry, the Beloved Country* (New York: Chas. Scribner's Sons, 1948), p. 89.

he rose to speak in the home church at Dallas. He loved the people and they loved him. This time everyone knew that he had just passed through Gethsemane, and that without defeat. One of the church members afterward reported: "His voice! I never shall forget his voice that morning, as we heard for the first time the note of sadness and pathos, which we now know so well. It seemed to carry the burden of all the grief in the world." [5] Much the same note sounds out from Alan Paton's novel concerning strife and forgiveness in South Africa. After his wayward son has been hanged Father Kumalo declares:

> Pain and suffering, they are a secret. Kindness and love, they are a secret. But I have learned that kindness and love can pay for pain and suffering. . . .
> I have never thought that a Christian would be free of suffering. . . . For our Lord suffered. And I come to believe that he suffered, not to save us from suffering, but to teach us how to bear suffering. For He knew that there is no life without suffering.[6]

5. SPEAKING IN A NATURAL WAY

In the pulpit, as elsewhere, be natural. Be your best self. In the past every worthy expositor has spoken in a fashion nearly all his own. Still there is a sense in which all first-class expositors have seemed alike in their forms of public address. Without exception they have excelled in the art of "animated conversation." This means enthusiasm in talking things over with the hearers. It means using all the charm, the variety, and the winsomeness that mark spirited talk at its best. Here stands no dictator sending down pontifical deliverances from some Olympian height, no advocate at the bar defending the Bible as

---

[5] See Powhatan W. James, *George W. Truett: A Biography* (Rev. ed.; New York: The Macmillan Co., 1945), p. 89.

[6] Paton, *op. cit.*, p. 222.

though it were about to be executed. Here speaks a friend, opening up a truth that he has discovered in the Book, and meeting a need that he has found among the people. To this kind of friend, as to his Lord, the common people listen gladly. Just now such a pastor is speaking to his friends about Acts 8:26-40.

THE GUIDANCE OF THE SPIRIT IN PERSONAL WORK

I. The Holy Spirit chooses the personal worker.
    A. Sometimes a minister; usually a layman
    B. A man already engaged in the Lord's work
II. The Spirit singles out the person to be won.
    A. Perhaps a stranger, as here; sometimes a brother
    B. Almost always a person of the same sex
III. The Spirit brings the two persons together.
    A. Where they can talk quietly
    B. Where the other can open up his heart
IV. The Spirit guides in the conversation.
    A. Here it concerns the Bible and Christ.
    B. Always it should be friendly; no debate.
V. The Spirit leads to a personal decision. Not always at once, but sometimes so, as here.
    A. Personal acceptance of Christ as Saviour
    B. Uniting with the church by baptism

In our day the majority of the men and women who join on confession of faith do so because of personal work. That in turn comes largely because of "animated conversation" led by the friend in the pulpit. In former years he may have exhorted the people to engage in soul winning, and scolded them if they did not respond. Now he strives to persuade. Using Deacon Philip as a living object lesson, the pastor may show how the Lord guides a personal worker like the friend in the pew. This kind of purpose does not call for oratory that dazzles with brilliance like that of the aurora borealis, or profundity that astonishes the saints with the weight of the pastor's erudition. The end in view leads the minister to engage in "co-operative preaching." This means to speak naturally, each time at one's best.

6. MAKING THE CHIEF POINTS STAND OUT

In any sort of teaching sermon a man wishes a few things to stand out boldly. He knows that the hearers cannot remember everything, but he wishes them to carry away something. Hence the sermon proceeds by stages as clearly marked as in the four stanzas of the hymn, "Come, Thou Almighty King." There the first stanza voices a prayer to God the Father; the second, to God the Son; the third, to God the Spirit; and the fourth, to God the "One in Three." Without some sort of careful planning the "animated conversation" of the man in the pulpit might have no more clearly marked stages than the desultory talk of friends resting out on the lawn.

Through what stages, for example, would the spiritual guide take his friends in preaching about "The Conversion of Public Enemy Number One"? The pastor would have in view the transformation of Saul from the chief of sinners to the noblest of saints, from the persecutor of the Church to the ambassador of Christ (Acts 9:1-18). How can the speaker make this conversion seem the most important event in church history, after the Day of Pentecost? Better still, how can he help to bring about such a conversion today? According to the record the conversion of Saul came through certain stages:

I. A meeting with Christ (vss. 1-9)
II. A prayer for light (vs. 11)
III. An interview with a believer (vss. 10-16)
IV. A leading of the Holy Spirit (vss. 17-18)

Among these four stages the first and the last stand out as most important. Both of them have to do with God. Conversion, as we all should know, begins and ends with God, but it does not take place in a vacuum. Between the meeting with the Living Christ and the enduement by the Holy Spirit note Saul's prayer for light and his coming to the light through a man whom Saul has never seen. How divine, and yet how human! The Lord does not always change a man's heart and life in exactly this way, but He always stands ready to do what we mortals cannot even attempt. Then He leaves us to do all that we can accomplish by His grace.

Various aspects of Christian conversion appeared in a series by a popular Philadelphia pastor on the theme, "This Business of Being Converted." In preparing a series of the sort anyone can find in the Acts more than enough cases to show various ways in which the Lord guides men who turn to Him. In each sermon of the series how can the preacher make "this business" seem the most important on earth? Partly by what we know as delivery. This refers to the way a man conducts a group of friends through a succession of intellectual and emotional experiences until at length they come to a certain decision.

Let us think of the matter in terms of music.[7] Leopold Stokowski or Sir Thomas Beecham plans to conduct an orchestra in rendering the *Ninth Symphony* by Beethoven. The maestro thinks of the first and the last movements as the most important. Still he wishes the second and the third to stand out in ways distinctly their own. He does not stop being a musician to make prosaic announcements about "firstly," "secondly," "thirdly," and "fourthly." Still he makes each of the four movements clear and, to a musician, memorable. The conductor secures these effects in ways that only a master of music can

[7] The suggestion comes from Arthur J. Gossip, *In Christ's Stead* (New York: George H. Doran Co., 1925), p. 64.

devise, and only a lover of music can discern. Should not a man in the pulpit deal as carefully and expertly with the symphony of God's transforming grace?

7. PREPARING TO PREACH WITHOUT NOTES

Almost without exception the ablest expository preachers have spoken with few notes, or else none. At Broadway Tabernacle in New York City, William M. Taylor read the expository sermons that later appeared as *The Parables of Our Saviour* and *The Miracles of Our Saviour.* In New York City and in London, John Henry Jowett read his sermons, including expository discourses on I Peter. He could read superbly, with the paragraph as a unit, so that he needed to glance at his paper only occasionally. Robertson took into the pulpit a few notes, at which he almost never glanced. Maclaren and G. Campbell Morgan, like the majority of other gifted expositors, have felt that anything in the way of manuscript or notes would interfere with the sort of eye contact that always marks "animated conversation" in its upper reaches. In order to speak without notes the expositor makes the basic framework of the sermon so simple that he can see it all with ease. For example, anyone can remember the following plan, which centers round the persons in Acts 10:1-33.

A BIBLE CURE FOR RACE PREJUDICE

One of the most serious problems today

A case that shows a Bible cure
I. Lack of race prejudice in a Roman (vss. 1-8). One of the N.T. centurions, all of them pleasing.
  A. One who loves the Lord
  B. One who treats Jews as equals
II. Lack of race prejudice in a Jew (vss. 9-16). More of a struggle here.
  A. A vision of human brotherhood

B. An opening of eyes to duty

III. Lack of race prejudice in a meeting (vss. 17-33). Understanding comes through action.

  A. A willingness to worship together

  B. A readiness to live together

This kind of brotherhood comes through the Spirit.

The resulting sermon would follow the stages in the chapter, but not in a wooden way. In the delivery the stages would stand out in the speaker's mind so clearly that he would not need to glance at any road map of his own making. As for the message, the basic truths all appear in the chapter. The record points to strong men in action, men like those who listen to the sermon. Both the centurion and the apostle Peter win their way into our hearts. When they meet together as brethren in the Lord, they show the ideal for all of us today. How can the local pastor promote interracial brotherhood more surely than by preaching from this chapter, and by making the most prominent parts stand out so boldly that the hearer will see them vividly and remember them forever?

> Join hands, then, brothers of the faith,
> Whate'er your race may be.
> Who serves my Father as a son
> Is surely kin to me.[8]

Expository sermons lend themselves readily to the method of preaching without notes. The effectiveness does not depend on tricks of oratory or on skill in coining epigrams. The speaker wishes rather to present the truth clearly and strongly, as Peter did in the house of Cornelius. As always elsewhere in the preaching of the apostles,[9] Peter followed a simple plan of his own

---

[8] From a hymn by John Oxenham, "No East or West" (1908).

[9] See Charles H. Dodd, *The Apostolic Preaching and Its Developments* (New York: Harper & Bros., 1950).

making. Of course he employed no notes. Like the prophets and the Lord Jesus the apostle spoke from heart to heart, and from eye to eye. In a sense "there is nothing new under the sun" (Eccl. 1:9c, Goodspeed), but not until comparatively modern times did ministers in large numbers begin to preach with manuscripts or notes.

Old-fashioned biblical ideas about the best way to speak in public have received striking confirmation from recent experiences with television. According to experts in this form of communication, "anyone seen reading from a manuscript loses his audience appeal." To a smaller degree the same holds true about the use of notes. At recent national political conventions experts in television brought out a device to help any huntsman who lacked courage and skill enough to "shoot without a rest." The machine consisted of "a black box with a sort of pianoplayer inside it, and containing in black letters the words of a speech." This device soon became known as "The Idiot's Board." [10]

8. PROCEEDING AT A MODERATE PACE

A teaching minister plans to speak more deliberately than his inspirational brother. Better still, the same man proceeds more slowly when he wishes to teach than when he seeks to inspire. Of course one could go too far in either direction. Any sort of delivery that calls attention to itself, either by excessive speed or by needless delays, probably goes too far. Somewhere between breathless haste and exasperating pauses there lies a golden mean. Within the sermon, as in a symphony, each main movement calls for a tempo more or less its own, either faster or slower than the others. At the time of delivery no spokesman for God ought to think about slowness or speed. Outside

---

[10] See the *Philadelphia Inquirer*, July 8, 1952.

the pulpit every "master of assemblies" can school himself to let the rate of his utterance accord with the spirit of what he is saying.

The mood of the man in the pulpit soon communicates itself to his friends in the pews. If he has mastered the subject, as well as himself, he can guide their thinking without worry or hurry or nervous tension. On the contrary, if he shows a sense of strain in struggling to grasp something he cannot see, or in trying to communicate excitement he does not feel, sensitive hearers will wish that they could turn a knob and stop the show. All this and more any minister can learn by listening to the radio and by watching television.

Let us think of a concrete case. A mature minister has an opportunity to preach twenty-five minutes at the induction of a younger pastor. The speaker wishes to open up an appropriate passage, such as Acts 10:24-48, which shows "The Ideal Church for Today." In this record about Peter at the home of Cornelius the visiting divine sees the sort of congregation that he hopes the young brother will help to build up in the next few years. Here again, the stress in the Bible record falls on persons in action. The passage suggests as an ideal for today a local church with:

I. A minister like Peter (vss. 24-29)
   A. Responds to the call of God
   B. Follows the guidance of the Spirit
   C. Shows a new feeling of humility
II. Lay leaders like Cornelius (vss. 30-33a)
   A. A man who prays before he acts
   B. Gives as freely as he prays
   C. Lives in the spirit of faith
III. People like those in Caesarea (vss. 33b-48)
   A. Come to church on time (vs. 33b)
   B. Hear the Word of God gladly (vss. 34-43)
   C. Receive the Holy Spirit (vss. 44-48)

Only a master could handle all of this material in twenty-five minutes. If anyone else made the attempt, he might rush through and leave behind him only an impression of nervous tension and "excited utterance." If anyone has mastered "the fine art of omission," he can take time to make the main ideas stand out memorably. Otherwise he may do well to speak about only one of the three main sections, perhaps the last one. Through days to come the people should look back on this address because they remember something to help them become more nearly an ideal church. "Now therefore we are all here present in the sight of God, to hear all that you have been commanded by the Lord" (10:33b).

What does the intelligent hearer remember about a sermon? When he listens to a pulpit orator, the layman recalls the speaker, especially his delivery. The man who hears a sermonizer recalls the sermon, perhaps as a work of art. The one who listens to an expositor should carry away the main ideas of the message, as it concerns the Lord and his own heart. Early in his pastoral life a minister ought to determine his main objective as a preacher. "Whenever I enter the pulpit shall I aim to exalt my Saviour, my sermon, or myself?" If the young man determines to exalt the Lord, and to do so by preaching from the Bible, then he should learn to speak deliberately, so that the hearer will remember what he should never forget.

Once I spoke about this matter before a group of churchmen. At the close of the address one of the laymen looked up with a twinkle in his eye and asked, "Don't you know that there is a fourth group, larger than those other three put together?"

"What group is that?"

"You say that one time we remember the speaker, the next time the sermon, and the third time the Saviour. When we laymen hear most of you preach, we do not remember anything except a big oblong blur."

If the man in the pulpit has something to say, why do the laymen not remember? Usually because the minister has not learned how to deliver his message so as to make the memorable parts stand out as boldly as the main headings on the first page of the morning newspaper.

9. SPEAKING IN TWO DIFFERENT WAYS

Every minister should know how to speak so as to teach, and at a different time, so as to inspire. During our national political conventions of 1952 millions of people heard over the radio and saw over television a succession of politicians who did not know how to speak, and occasionally a person who had mastered the art. A certain United States senator excelled in two sorts of delivery. In one address he explained a difficult subject, which the hearers did not begin to understand. He wished them to see the facts as he understood them, and then to vote a certain way. Hence he spoke deliberately, and made the chief points stand out as boldly as though he had been a first-class expository preacher.

In his other address the statesman wished to inspire enthusiasm for a certain candidate, and not to explain anything special. Hence he spoke more quickly, though not at breakneck speed. He did not make the successive stages of the address stand out boldly. Neither way of speaking would have suited the other address. In all these matters a wise man first determines what he wishes to accomplish. Then he plans to speak so as to secure the response he desires. If he wishes to teach, he schools himself to speak deliberately, with more or less appeal to the intellect. Like his Maker the interpreter seems to say, "Come now, let us reason together" (Isa. 1:18a). A man who reasons does not rush as though he were running to witness a fire and felt afraid that it might die out before he arrived.

On the other hand, the public speaker who wishes to inspire

tends to speak more quickly and feelingly. Without losing self-control he appeals to emotion more than to thought. Since he does not voice ideas that call for the use of much brain power, he can move along at a brisk rate, though he should never become incoherent or seem breathless. If any minister will learn to prepare and deliver these two sorts of sermons, he should find no difficulty in securing a hearing for either kind of message from God. Of course this account makes the facts seem too simple. In the pulpit during any one sermon a minister tends to use both forms of public address. Even so, the popular effectiveness of each part depends on skill in making the style of the delivery accord with the spirit of the message.

In many of these matters confirmation comes from an unexpected source. In *The King's Story,* the Duke of Windsor tells about his first attempts at public speaking after he became the Prince of Wales:

The more appearances I had to make, the more I came to respect the really first-class speech as one of the highest human accomplishments. No one I knew seemed to possess that rare and envied gift of speaking well in so high a degree as Mr. Winston Churchill, who was a sympathetic witness of some of my earliest attempts. "If you have an important point to make," he advised at the outset of my career, "don't try to be subtle and clever about it. Use the pile driver. Hit the point once, then come back and hit it again, and then hit it the third time—a tremendous whack!" [11]

[11] New York: G. P. Putnam's Sons, 1950, p. 137.

CHAPTER NINE

THE QUESTIONS FROM AN OPEN FORUM

NOW THAT WE HAVE THOUGHT ABOUT PRACTICAL WAYS and means of preparing expository sermons, we ought to consider certain questions. The ones that follow have come to me again and again. Others that I pass by have come only occasionally. The ones below should help to bring out features I have not stressed, at least not enough. In writing a book, as in teaching a class, practical theology calls for give-and-take. The taking has not usually consisted of criticism; but when that has come, it has helped me to make things clear, and to guide me in using cases. The answers here do not aim to prove anything, attack any person, or disparage any system. They should encourage the nonexpository preacher to begin doing this kind of pulpit work at intervals, and hearten the experienced interpreter to keep on, every Lord's Day, in a fashion all his own. Now come the questions from the floor.

1. DODGING THE DIFFICULT

"Why do you dodge the difficult books and subjects? You make this kind of pulpit work seem easy." To a large extent the implied criticism seems to me valid. It came to me first from a distinguished seminary professor. In a review otherwise favorable he pointed out this aspect of my *Preaching from the Bible*. In the original manuscript the chapter about "The [Bible] Book Sermon" dealt with Job, Ecclesiastes, and Proverbs. That discussion did not make a book sermon seem easy to prepare, as it is not. The editors thought the treatment too heavy for the man in view. So I substituted other examples, less difficult. The continued appeal of the book seems to have confirmed the judgment of the editors. Personally, I have seldom found more satisfaction in the pulpit than when preaching about the problem in the book of Job, or Ecclesiastes. Still I do not recommend the project to an inexperienced expositor. I hope that in time he will learn to swim in deep waters.

For another reason I sometimes seem to dodge the difficult. The lay hearers now in view have not been exposed to expository preaching. With some exceptions people will listen more eagerly and receive more help if the minister preaches occasionally about a simple psalm, or a parable—it may be a scene from the life of Joseph or Paul—than if the inexperienced expositor tries to expound difficult passages from the first part of Romans or Ephesians. However, when an experienced expositor comes in course to a difficult passage, such as Phil. 2:5-11, he should not dodge. He will find that the harder the going the greater the joy of achievement. Also he will discover that most people can follow anything he can make clear and helpful. Often we underestimate the capacity of God's people to digest sermonic food.

A third reason may not seem so valid. Some of the most glorious truths and passages of the Bible do not lend themselves readily to expository treatment. For example, think of Christian doctrines. I believe strongly in the Deity of Christ, the personality of the Holy Spirit, and the resurrection of the believer. I feel that every pastor should accept these New Testament teachings and tell his people why. He should not argue, or try to prove, but rather explain and illuminate, with "sweet reasonableness." During my joyous years in the pastorate I aimed to do expository preaching once every Lord's Day. Also

I often dealt with Christian doctrines, usually at night. I do not remember to have done so in an expository sermon.

For instance, take the subject, "Why Believe in the Resurrection?" The answer may come from the words of Paul to King Agrippa: "Why is it thought incredible by any of you that God raises the dead?" (Acts 26:8.) A man who thinks ought to believe in the resurrection because he believes in God. This sentence has to do with Christian belief in general: "It all depends on how great a God one believes in." So said one of the world's most distinguished astronomers, Dr. Henry Norris Russell, of Princeton University. Speaking colloquially, he replied to an officious woman who asked how he as a foremost scientist could believe in God, and serve as a ruling elder in the Presbyterian Church. In response to a letter of inquiry about the matter Dr. Russell wrote: "It would represent me more accurately to say, 'Madam, that depends on how great a God one believes in, and on whether one can trust Him regardless of changing theories about details.'"

In preaching about tremendous doctrines a pastor may prefer to work textually or topically. The same holds true in dealing with certain golden chapters, each of them as a whole. The chapter limits may not always coincide with the arrangement in our Bibles today. Many of the greatest chapters lend themselves to expository uses. Others do not, at least not easily. In the list that follows I have preached from nearly all of the chapters, each as a unit, but not from Gen. 1, Isa. 40, and Rev. 21. From these wondrous passages I have preached in other ways, equally biblical.

Any pastor who wishes to promote home use of the Bible may ask the people for lists of their favorite chapters. He may begin with lists of beloved psalms, six or eight, and then use them in a series, "Psalms Our People Love." After an interval of time he may ask for lists of favorite chapters in John or in

Isaiah. After the minister has trained the people to respond, he may call for a master list, covering the entire Bible. In two congregations and at two seminaries I asked my friends to select twenty golden chapters. The results appear below, with two alternate passages for young people. At least for the present, many of them prefer Isa. 6 rather than 40, and Rom. 12 rather than 8. The list aims to include chapters about all the supreme truths of the Christian faith. It would be much too long for use in a series, but still it provides one of the most attractive forms of adult Bible education.

CHAPTERS OUR PEOPLE LOVE

Selected by our people and compiled by our secretary

Gen. 1—The Creation of the World
Exod. 20—The Basic Law of Our God
Ps. 23—The Psalm of the Good Shepherd
Ps. 103—The Lovingkindness of the Father
Ps. 121—The Psalm of the Traveling Man
Isa. 6—The Young Man at Worship (for y.p.)
Isa. 40—The Gospel of Divine Power
Isa. 53—The Sufferings of Our Saviour
Isa. 55—The Gospel in the Old Testament
Matt. 5-7—The Practical Side of the Kingdom
Luke 2—The Birth of Our Redeemer
Luke 15—The Joys of Finding the Lost
John 1—The Background of the Gospel
John 14—The Secret of Untroubled Hearts
John 15—The Christian Source of Fruitfulness
Acts 2—The Power of the Holy Spirit
Rom. 8—The Riches of God's Grace
Rom. 12—The Daily Lives of Believers (y.p.)
I Cor. 13—The Greatness of Christian Love
I Cor. 15—The Glory of the Resurrection
Heb. 11—The Heroes of the Faith
Rev. 21—The Final Victory of Our Lord

2. RECOMMENDING OTHER METHODS

"Why do you recommend other ways of preaching from the Bible?" Largely because God has blessed other ways of using divine truth in meeting human needs. Sometimes in our zeal we advocates of expository work claim too much. From the history of preaching we should learn that the value of any message does not depend on the homiletical methods of the preacher, but on the truth he declares and on the way he uses it to help the hearers. If anyone wishes to deal textually with "The Gospel That Sets Men Free" (John 8:32), or topically with "The Holy Spirit as Our Teacher" (John 16:13), who should find fault? On the other hand, the history of the Church, as in the days of Chrysostom and Augustine, or of Luther and Calvin, shows that God's people gain much from the exposition of Bible units longer than isolated verses.

Experience also shows, as we have seen, that the expository method does not lend itself equally well to all sorts of purposes. In general it appeals more to church members who attend regularly than to the unchurched and the unsaved. Some expositors, but not many, may have excelled as soul winners. The most effective evangelists, such as Spurgeon and Moody, have stressed either the text or the topic, usually the text. As Spurgeon used to say, "It is the text and not the sermon that saves the sinner." For instance, turn to Eph. 2:8: "By grace you have been saved through faith; and this is not your own doing, it is the gift of God." In quoting the text a minister need not thump the prepositions, but in preaching a sermon he ought to make clear the distinction between *by* and *through*. The power to save rests with God. The working of the power depends on the hearer. Salvation, by grace, through faith. Without taking time to explain the surrounding paragraph the evangelist has his hands full enough if he deals with this one verse alone, and uses it in leading the hearer to accept the Saviour.

I recommend other ways of preaching, also, for the sake of variety. A ten-talent man, like Maclaren in his later years, or G. Campbell Morgan in his glory, may do nothing but expository work month after month. If a less gifted interpreter did so, his pulpit work might suffer from lack of variety. According to Bishop Fred P. Corson, of the Methodist Church in the Philadelphia area, laymen often object to the pastor's sermons because of sameness. During any one week a wise man lets no two sermons assume the same form, because they do not meet the same needs. From week to week, also, he plans to keep away from the sort of sameness that calls attention to itself, unpleasantly. One way to secure wholesome variety is to preach at times in ways not expository. Cultivate what Spurgeon called "the surprise power."

3. OVERLAPPING WITH SUNDAY SCHOOL

"How can I prevent overlapping with the Sunday school?" A wise question, not easy to answer. On any one Lord's Day in a school with departmental graded lessons the pupils take up various parts of the Bible. In order to avoid duplication the pastor needs to think about the biblical content of the lessons in the adult department, and perhaps among the young people. In deciding what to preach during any period a wise man keeps away from parts of the Bible where adult members of the school will be working. On the other hand, most pastors have found to their sorrow that they cannot rely on the church school as the sole educational agency of the local church. For one reason, alas, many adult members do not attend the Sunday school.

Even in treating the same passage of Scripture the methods of the pulpit expositor ought to differ from those of an expert Bible school teacher. The pastor ought to think of his expository sermon as an act of worship. He should come into the pulpit to reveal a truth from God, a truth that the hearer ought to receive so as to live in its light. The Sunday-school teacher, on the other hand, should not serve mainly as a leader of worship. He ought to explain and illuminate a Bible passage, both as a whole and in its parts; it may be verse by verse. As a rule he should not lecture but use a discussion method. So he should lead the pupils to understand a chosen part of Genesis, or Luke. As for teaching or preaching without biblical content, that does not concern us now.

Often the duplication comes from the church school, not from the pastor. Instead of serving as a school, the teaching department of the congregation tends to become a substitute for the main sanctuary. This holds true especially of the Men's Bible Class. Think of opening exercises, a lay sermon, and closing exercises. In the adult department of many schools the order of the service and most of the details resemble morning worship. The more the officers and teachers admire their minister the more do they tend to change the teaching branch of the local church into a place for worship under the leadership of amateurs. Then the leaders of the home church wonder why many people choose between Sunday school and morning worship.

In view of these conditions, all too common, what can the pastor do? As the spiritual leader of the congregation he can gradually bring about a reform, so that the school will become a school. The distinction between a teaching agency and a place for worship may not stand out clearly on paper, but it will become clear to anyone who attends a Friday evening service in a Jewish synagogue and later visits the school in the commodious building next door. In a Christian church why should people not come together at nine-thirty to learn the ways of God, and at eleven o'clock to worship the King? Morning worship ought to include a sermon far more like the words of an apostle or a prophet than like the inspiring chalk-talk of a Bible school teacher who employs a discussion method. So let the church become a church, and the school remain a school.[1]

4. STRESSING THE OLD TESTAMENT

"Why do you recommend so much preaching from the Old Testament?" For various reasons, not least because the Old Testament is the most important part of the Bible, except the New. Also because the Old Testament is even less understood. No pastor or people can begin to know or appreciate the New Testament without some knowledge and appreciation of the Old. As for the proportion between the sermons from the Old and those from the New, it is hard to find a happy medium. An interesting suggestion comes from a wise English bishop with previous experience as a missionary leader in India. As a working standard the bishop recommends that 25 per cent of a pastor's sermons come from the Old Testament, 40 per cent from the Gospels, and 25 per cent from the remainder of the New Testament, with 10 per cent of free time for special sermons. Then he utters a word of caution, all the more welcome since it comes from a bishop: "In such a matter, there are no rules, only certain principles." [2] In much the same spirit I recommend 40 per cent from the Old Testament, 30 from the Gospels, and 30 from the remainder of the New Testament, with no free time for anything but biblical preaching.

[1] See Nevin C. Harner, *The Educational Work of the Church* (New York and Nashville: Abingdon-Cokesbury Press, 1939), Ch. V.

[2] Stephen C. Neill, *Fulfill Thy Ministry* (New York: Harper & Bros., 1952), p. 67; a wise book, full of truth and light.

Here again a pastor must watch for variety. Otherwise he may fall into a rut of his own making. One man keeps mainly to the Gospels. Another preaches often from the Epistles, or the Apocalypse. A third, perhaps from Scotland, relies largely on the Old Testament, with its drama. In any of these cases a study of the people and their needs might show the wisdom of ranging more widely over various parts of Holy Writ. Surely no interpreter should neglect the Old Testament, the only Bible the Lord Jesus knew in the days of His flesh. Neither should anyone pass by the Apocalypse, which James Denney once described as the most Christian book in the Bible. Except for the first three chapters the young interpreter had better feed the sheep for a while in pastures less Alpine. Whatever the reasons, expository preachers in the past have done much of their best work in opening up the Old Testament.

5. FOLLOWING THE CHRISTIAN YEAR

"To what extent should my sermons follow the Christian Year?" Largely, but not slavishly. In the Lutheran Church, as in the Protestant Episcopal, Bible passages are prescribed for public reading, and are optional for pulpit uses. A wise man makes the most out of all these options. On almost every Lord's Day he preaches from one of the lessons, or from a pericope. With all due honor for *The Book of Common Prayer*, and for like masterpieces of sacred art, I believe that in most liturgical churches the clergymen need to make a careful study of expository preaching. So do we all.

"What of the pastor whose church does not prescribe any series of Scripture readings, or even send out an optional lectionary?" For his own sake and that of his people let him borrow, adapt, or devise a lectionary of his own. Then he can lead the people through the Bible, stage by stage, every year, so that they will come face to face with the major truths and duties of our holy faith. A diligent worker may follow a different lectionary every year, with some of the most majestic passages recurring annually. First in the study and then in the pulpit the minister can deal with passages that show the unfolding of the mightiest drama in world history, the drama of our redemption.[3]

During Advent a pastor may have three sermons from the book of Micah. After the first one he may ask the people to read this prophetic book, with a warning about the difficulty of understanding the first chapter. In the sermons from Micah the stress may fall on "The Gospel of the Common People." The purpose, of course, relates to the coming celebration of the Incarnation. The three sermons: "The Religion of the Practical Man" (6:8), "The Bible Vision of World Peace" (4:1-4), and "The Gospel from Bethlehem" (5:2). A year later the sermons may come from Isa. 1–12, and so on from year to year. In time the people should begin to feel at home in the most difficult and the most important part of the Old Testament world—the most important, except the Psalms—because it has to do with the coming of Christ and His Kingdom.[4]

The Sunday before Christmas may call for a sermon about "The Heart of the Christmas Gospel" (Matt. 1:18-23). The Sunday after Christmas, "Wise Men Still Worship" (Matt. 2:1-12). In connection with these opening sermons from Matthew the pastor may invite his lay friends to read in their homes "The Gospel of the Kingdom." He should encourage them to find what each paragraph tells about Christ Jesus. Unless someone guides lay readers, they may become so engrossed with John

---

[3] For a fuller discussion see my *Planning a Year's Pulpit Work* (New York and Nashville: Abingdon-Cokesbury Press, 1942).

[4] See my *Preaching from Prophetic Books* (New York and Nashville: Abingdon-Cokesbury Press, 1951).

the Baptist, Peter, and other men, as to give the Lord Jesus a secondary place. In making plans for the season the minister ought also to save time for messages from the latter part of the Gospel (16:13–28:20), by far the most important part. In four years he can preach here and there from each of the Gospels, all by itself. As for the fifth year, and thereafter, he can go through the same Bible fields once again, preaching from still other paragraphs with their inexhaustible riches.

After Easter, slightly ignoring chronology, the interpreter may preach from the Book of the Acts, where he should stress the Living Christ, or the Holy Spirit. A year later, from First Corinthians, or one of the other less difficult epistles. During the summer he may help to avert a slump in church attendance and interest. By preaching from the Psalms and from the Parables he can make the Bible seem a contemporary book. For two successive summers, two months each time, I have occupied the pulpit of a large Methodist church nearby. The friends in charge of the publicity have stressed the preaching of expository sermons, one year from the Psalms and the parables in Luke, the next year from the miracles in Mark and the parables in Matthew. The attendance and the interest have more than justified the experiment.

Starting anew in the autumn the pastor may work in an Old Testament book, such as Judges. Or he may single out a portion of a longer book, such a portion as Gen. 37–50, or Exod. 1–20. Here again the interpreter ought to stress the divine as well as the human. In preaching about *Personalities of the Old Testament* [5] never become so concerned about Joseph or Samuel as to ignore or minimize God. Do not stress *Human Nature in the Bible* [6] so much as divine grace in deal-

[5] See Fleming James, title as above (New York: Chas. Scribner's Sons, 1939).

[6] See William Lyon Phelps, title as above (New York: Chas. Scribner's Sons, 1922).

ing with a man like the one in the pew. On the other hand, do not talk about God as a theoretical "Wholly Other" who dwells on some distant star and serves as an absentee Landlord. Preach about "the God of Abraham, the God of Isaac, the God of Jacob" (Exod. 3:15b), preferably one at a time. As Pascal insists, preach far more about the God of Jesus Christ.

This way of preaching throughout the Christian Year differs from other methods chiefly in one respect. The emphasis here falls on use of the Bible the way it was written, book by book, and, within each book, unit by unit. How else can both pastor and people come to know the Bible so well?

6. PREACHING ON SPECIAL DAYS

"What should I preach on special days?" First pray for special grace and for practical wisdom. Here in the States some congregations have become half "dazed" by observance of special days, some of them secular and most of them sentimental. At most churches the decline in attendance begins soon after Easter, when many of us practically quit preaching the Gospel and begin discussing all sorts of related matters. Every pastor ought to welcome a special day that calls for a message about God, the Holy Spirit, or the Trinity. As for humanitarian movements, good in themselves, he ought to keep on the main track of Christianity. When some secular issue calls for a hearing from the pulpit, he should resolve with the leader of old: "I am doing a great work and I cannot come down. Why should the work stop while I leave it and come down to you?" (Neh. 6:3.)

"What if local traditions call for special sermons about causes not distinctly Christian?" In any such case a wise man co-operates with the lay officers, graciously. If they wish him to deliver a certain special sermon, he does so, willingly, and takes the message from the Bible. In two different parishes where the officers wished special morning sermons on nine or ten Sundays, I never found it impossible to preach them from Holy Writ. Unfortunately, most of these special days come during spring and early summer, when the pastor ought to be preaching from a major book of the Bible. Ordinarily one can deal with any special cause by using a passage from the book in hand. If not, he can lay it aside, not without a sigh. No one has yet completely solved the problem of what to do about preaching on special days.

Some of these occasions a pastor welcomes. Among them stands out the Sunday before Thanksgiving, a day distinctly Protestant. Suppose that through the fall he has been preaching from Judges. On the Sunday before Thanksgiving he may give the last of these sermons. Better still, he may turn to the Book of Ruth. Benjamin Franklin used to refer to this little romance as the most beautiful short story ever written—a story all the more appealing because it is true. The book seems to have come from the same era as Judges. If so, the love story shows that even in the most troublous times the blessing of God may come to a rural community through a mature woman like Naomi, and a country gentleman like Boaz. The message about the "little town of Bethlehem" will lead up to Advent sermons about the Babe of Bethlehem. Ruth 1:16-17 provides a keynote for the message at Thanksgiving time.

LOYALTY TO GOD IN HUMAN RELATIONS

Loyalty here means love in everyday action.
  I. In loving a mother-in-law (ch. 1)
 II. In dealing with men (ch. 2)
III. In finding a mate (ch. 3)
 IV. In making a home (ch. 4)
The conclusion has to do with Christ's birth.

7. PUZZLING ABOUT THE EVENING SERVICE

"What can I do about the evening service?" If at all possible, I should have one the year round. During a recent speaking engagement among Southern Baptists in Alabama I found that in Birmingham and its environs they have 104 churches, and that every one of those churches holds an evening service twelve months in the year. In congregations elsewhere, not Baptist, the hour has shifted to 4:00 or 5:00 P.M. Any hour will serve, especially if it remains fixed. Attending the "second service," or not attending, becomes a matter of habit. Those in charge need to remember that the tone color of public worship should vary according to the hour of the day.

I believe that almost every community where enough people live would support the right sort of evening service, or vespers. If so, the second service needs to differ from the one earlier in the day. At present we shall think only about the preaching. Plan to do popular expository work in the morning, and not at night, or else vice versa. In fields here and there over the land people respond both morning and evening when they have wholesome variety of pulpit fare. If so, the pastor must work as hard in preparing the evening sermon as for the one in the morning.

For reasons unknown a series at night usually attracts more attention than one in the morning. A Methodist pastor may preach for a month about "The Gospel in the Hymns of Charles Wesley." If the series comes to an end after Thanksgiving, he may close with "Hark! The Herald Angels Sing." The stress would not fall on the writer of the song, or the composer of the tune, but on the content of the hymn. Like almost every other hymn by Charles Wesley, this one consists of Christian doctrine set to music. "The Gospel That Sings." If anyone asks what this kind of evening message has to do with expository preaching, let him examine the five stanzas of our simplest hymn about the Cross. In order to tell boys and girls why the Saviour died, a young Irish gentlewoman wrote "There Is a Green Hill Far Away." The headings below indicate the content of the successive stanzas. The resulting sermon explains the hymn. The alliteration may help the hearer to remember, but the pastor should not often use this device.

THE SIMPLICITY OF THE CROSS

I. The place of the Cross (stanza 1)
II. The puzzle of the Cross (st. 2)
III. The purpose of the Cross (st. 3)
IV. The Prince on the Cross (st. 4)
V. The people of the Cross (st. 5)

A Presbyterian pastor near us had an evening series, semi-expository, about "The Gospel According to Bunyan." The young minister became so fascinated with *The Pilgrim's Progress* that he wished to share his findings with the people who came to church at night, and with other friends. So he prepared a number of evening sermons, all of them biblical in substance, centering round scenes in the world's noblest allegory. Over in Edinburgh, Alexander Whyte[7] and John Kelman[8] had done something of the kind. The local interpreter strove rather to show the meaning of Bunyan's immortal allegory in thought forms of his community today. He found the people eager to learn about the "Slough of Despond," "Doubting Castle," and "Giant Despair." Even if that series had not attracted a throng of hearers, it would have done untold

[7] See *Bunyan Characters in the Pilgrim's Progress,* 3 vols. (London, 1902).

[8] See *Road of Life, A Study of Pilgrim's Journey,* 2 vols. (New York: George H. Doran Co., n.d.).

good. "Nothing can hinder the Lord from saving by many or by few" (I Sam. 14:6d).

A related question concerns the wisdom of holding identical services at 8:30 and at 11:00 A.M. Many of us rejoice in the spread of this custom. We do not believe that Protestantism will continue to thrive locally on the basis of only one hour for public worship each Lord's Day. Sometimes we wonder about the wisdom of having two services identical. When has a man become a master preacher on the basis of one sermon a week? We think it much more nearly ideal to meet a different sort of needs, and in a different fashion, at each service. Unless a minister has histrionic powers, the repetition of the same prayers and the delivery of the same sermon may suffer at one service or the other. Why not make one sermon expository and the other one different? However, the plan of holding identical services has already done much to promote church attendance and interest.

As Protestants we ought frankly to recognize that there is nothing sacrosanct about certain hours for public worship. In a capital city a pastor recently became concerned about the religious illiteracy of many young married people loosely attached to the church. He found them ready to meet with him for what we may call popular expository studies of the Bible, though he employed a term less formidable. After a careful canvass by leaders among the young married people he discovered that he could get them together at only one time during the week, on Monday evening. Before the canvass he never had dreamed of Monday evening as the most available time. "New occasions teach new duties."

8. ADVISING ABOUT MIDWEEK WORSHIP

"What do you advise about midweek worship?" Whatever the field, I should hold some sort of religious service every week between Sundays. In a rural community during the winter, or in a downtown church, the service might come near the middle of the day. When at home I should lead the service myself. Except while on the annual vacation I should plan to be at home on this strategic day. If for a while it did not seem feasible to get a group of people together at the church, I should go out into various districts and hold informal cottage meetings. Before many months had gone I should hope to have a nucleus of praying folk, ready to gather with me at the church, or in the parsonage. The effectiveness of a midweek meeting depends in part on the room, its size, shape, and atmosphere. On the contrary, the midweek service has languished or died during the period when we church folk have devoted most attention to interior church architecture. We need to begin thinking more about being filled with the Spirit of God.

The service would consist of informal and spirited praise and prayer, leading up to equally informal and spirited discussion of a paragraph or two in a Bible book, such as Philippians. Both in spirit and in content the meeting should differ from anything else all week, and seem like family worship at its best. If the people wish to eat together at 6:00 P.M., for geographical and social reasons, very well, but the stress ought to be on free-for-all talks with the pastor about a Bible passage, in the spirit of prayer. This evening gathering may become known as "The Bible Hour," or else "The Pastor's Hour." Without seeming to lecture, or even to teach, he can lead the lay friends through a Bible book, stage by stage. To the paragraphs in Philippians he may devote six or eight Wednesday evening hours.

After a year or so he may feel ready to deal with the more difficult epistle to the Ephesians. Let us suppose that he has led in half an hour of family worship, with no long prayers or long readings. He has called for a number of familiar hymns, and has led in concert repetition of familiar verses from Paul. In various ways the pastor can encourage everyone present to take part. In order to promote a feeling of friendliness he does not stand behind a pulpit but on a level with the people, or else on a platform only a little higher than the floor. When he comes to the Bible period, he conducts a free-for-all conversation about an old-time letter. The people should feel ready to talk about the writer, the readers, and the message. In their homes they have been reading Ephesians, both at the family altar and elsewhere, always in the spirit of prayer.

The home readings begin after the introduction to Ephesians as a whole. A week later the pastor can take up the first paragraph or two. With the aid of a blackboard he can get the people to understand something about even the loftiest flights of the Apostle's faith. Better still, the minister can guide his friends in living according to these heaven-born ideals. Best of all, he can watch them grow in love for Christ and His Church. These results will come to the interpreter after hours of living with Paul's epistle, in the light of Eph. 5:25-27 as the key verse. The letter falls into these main sections:

THE GLORY OF CHRIST IN HIS CHURCH

I. The spiritual history of the church (chs. 1-3). The Christian philosophy of redemption
   A. God's part in salvation (ch. 1)
   B. Our part in salvation (ch. 1)
   C. The minister's part in salvation (ch. 3)
II. The practical duties of church members (chs. 4-6)
   A. In the local church (4:1-16)
   B. In social life (4:17–5:20)
   C. In the Christian home (5:21–6:9)
   D. In Christian warfare (6:10-20)

In a Southern city a Presbyterian pastor has for years led his people through the Bible, book by book. To each book he devotes as many Wednesday evenings as the facts seem to warrant. Why should he hurry through if the people wish to linger, or dawdle if they do not want to tarry? Partly because of an evening meal, served at cost, Wednesday has become known for its Church Night, with the Bible Hour as the climactic feature. On Thursday morning the church secretary mails out stenciled copies of what the pastor wishes his friends to remember about the ground they covered the evening before. In short, he works hard and uses all his brain power, especially his imagination.

These friends in the South have recently completed a new and commodious church building. When I visited them as a guest minister, I heard much more about their Wednesday evening meetings than about their new edifice. As for the pastor, he finds that the preparation for midweek worship keeps him close to the Written Word of God and brings him nearer to the hearts of the people. Instead of talking about "putting new life into the old prayer meeting," he thinks it better to put a spirit of Bible study into the present minister. As for some of these old prayer meetings, they ought to have been buried soon after they died.

9. ANNOUNCING THE PREACHING PROGRAM

"Do you think it wise to announce these preaching plans in advance?" In general, yes; in detail, no. I should want the people to know in advance any book of the Bible that I wished them to read for the next few weeks or months, but not the parts that I expected to take up in the pulpit. Of course I should announce and publicly stress any series, but not the parts in any regular course of expository sermons. A wise housemother plans to stress any special meal, but she does not at the beginning of the autumn hand out menus for the next six months. As a rule she wishes the other members of the household to know little or nothing about what to expect when they come to the dinner table. She says, "I keep them guessing."

A minister has a more serious reason for not announcing detailed pulpit plans far in advance. In our swiftly moving times, often kaleidoscopic, he cannot feel sure in detail about what he ought to preach six months from today. In August when he plans for the pulpit work of the coming year he knows that changing conditions may cause him to alter the course here and there. So he keeps the details to himself. In March or in May, if he has to revise the plans, he will need to make no explanations. Of course he finds it easier to change plans if he has in writing plans to change. In terms of the farm the need for minor changes should not keep any shepherd from making plans to feed the sheep in certain pastures. As a matter of fact, experienced pastors seldom feel much concern about this matter. They simply use common sense.

10. HEARING FROM THE TYPICAL LAYMAN

"To what extent does the typical layman desire expository sermons?" Here again we advocates often overstate our case. We may wish that the average church member would ask his minister for this kind of pulpit fare, but we ought to know that in the history of the pulpit the expository impulse has come from the minister, not from the hearers. At least that has been the experience of every expositor who has appeared in this book. In Brighton and in Manchester the people did not keep bombarding the pastor with demands for expository sermons. Why should laymen do so today? To whom does the Lord reveal His will about these holy concerns? To the pastor, not the people. What do many of them know or care about our homiletical labels and our ways of preparing sermons? If the pastor brings them heart-warming, soul-stirring, life-changing messages from God's Book, why should they ask for anything more? Let us not make them sermon-conscious, lest they become critical. On the other hand, if they come to church week after week hungering and thirsting for soul food, and then go away neither taught nor fed nor stirred, they may begin to say in their prayers: "Lord, next time send us a man who can preach."

Instead of demanding expository sermons some laymen may for a while not enjoy this kind of preaching. They have not learned to bring their brains to church and keep them busy there. They wish to possess their souls in peace, or else be wafted up into the stratosphere so as to capture the secrets of the stars. In the midst of people with motion-picture minds and television tendencies a man who believes in a teaching ministry may have to work six months before he gets the large majority of the hearers to relish pulpit expositions. If only for this reason he should know how to preach in other ways, and do so part of the time. Little by little, if he keeps on with expository sermons at times, most people will respond. Others will join the happy throng. Soon the lay friends may begin asking for more sermons from the Bible the way it was written.

11. FORECASTING THE FUTURE

"What do you think about the future of expository preaching?" I believe that here in the States there is more of it now than at any time in the present century, and I hope that the trend will increase. I do not think that expository fare will ever displace other sorts of pulpit food, but among pastors on the field and students in the seminary I sense a growing desire for mastery in pulpit exposition. Unfortunately I note that some of the seekers keep looking for a cookbook full of simple recipes for turning out all sorts of luscious viands. On the other hand, seekers after short cuts seem to be decreasing in number. The vast majority of ministers today are ready to work. They also know why James Black entitled his book *The Mystery of Preaching*.

The chief barrier to expository preaching comes from the work of the parish. If any pastor wishes to excel as a teaching minister, he must first solve the problem of local church leadership. Before he can find the time, and acquire the poise, necessary to interpret the Bible for human needs today, he must somehow organize and lead the home church as a going concern. He must also learn to say no to demands of zealous people who would drag him out of the study and set him at work serving tables (Acts 6:1-7; cf. Exod. 18:13-27). For this reason—because I felt sorry for young ministers called of God to preach from the Bible, and gradually becoming accustomed to running ecclesiastical merry-go-rounds—I wrote my book *Pastoral Leadership*.[9] With all my heart I believe that our laymen and laywomen will respond to the tactful leadership of a minister who wishes them to do the other work of the congregation and to set him free for his holy calling as pastor, preacher, and man of prayer.

So much for my opinions. They have come through watching all sorts of ministers at work, both in books about yesterday and on the field today. Let us not leave all these matters on the level of human opinion. I am neither inspired nor infallible. I cannot point to any modern book as a source of infallible guidance about what to preach, or how. Still we Christians do have a Supreme Court that never errs. In all these matters about preaching and allied concerns the Lord Jesus Christ stands ready to speak with final authority. He

---

[9] New York and Nashville: Abingdon-Cokesbury Press. 1949.

speaks through the Holy Spirit, and mainly through the Written Word. Surely Christ wishes us to preach from the Bible that makes Him known, and in ways that will make the Bible known.

Wherever the Lord Christ has His way in the pulpit of tomorrow, the people will be well fed, spiritually. They will be free from "a famine on the land; not a famine of bread, nor a thirst for water, but of hearing the words of the Lord" (Amos 8:11). As for ways and means of doing popular expository work, both today and tomorrow, the Lord Christ stands ready to guide and restrain through the Holy Spirit. "If any man's will is to do his will, he shall know whether the teaching is from God" (John 7:17a). This verse points to what Phillips Brooks calls "The Illumination of Obedience." From this point of view let us now consider the effect on the local pastor who learns how to excel as an expository preacher for today.

CHAPTER TEN

THE EFFECT UPON THE LOCAL PASTOR

E XPOSITORY PREACHING DOES MUCH FOR THE LOCAL pastor, who may be in need of help today. "For many years I have been convinced that the greatest need of the contemporary church is the strengthening of the local pulpit." [1] So says Dr. Ralph W. Sockman of New York City. He is explaining why he has chosen to remain a pastor, a radio preacher, and a seminary lecturer on preaching, instead of becoming a Methodist bishop. Dr. Theodore Otto Wedel, Canon of the Episcopal Cathedral at Washington, D.C., says much the same thing, negatively. As Warden of the College of Preachers for more than a decade he has had many opportunities to appraise current preaching. In an article on "The Lost Authority of the Pulpit" he asks a question that concerns us all:

Is the authority of the pulpit under a cloud in contemporary church life in America? Statistics are not available, and armchair indictments ought to be suspect. Yet evidence is not lacking that the Sunday sermon, still an institutionalized marvel of loyalty to tradition in our common life, occupies a place of less importance, in the eyes of both minister and people, than it did in the days of our fathers. One proof of the dwindling of its importance is fairly incontrovertible, namely, its comparative brevity when set alongside the sermon literature of previous generations. [2]

[1] *The Christian Century,* July 9, 1952, p. 808.
[2] See *Theology Today,* July, 1952, p. 165. See also the estimate of secular historians, Henry S. Commager, *The American Mind* (New Haven: Yale University Press, 1950), 167, 414, 443; D. W. Brogan, *The Price of Revolution* (New York: Harper & Bros., 1951), Ch. IV.

With both of these church leaders the rest of us agree. We ought to restore and enhance the authority and power of the local pulpit. When we ask "How?" we meet unexpected difficulties. Surely we ought not to throw the blame chiefly on the local pastor. Neither should we expect to find cheap and easy remedies for deep-seated ills. If time and opportunity permitted, a book of the present size might deal with the roots of the matter in the divinity school. Much weakness in the pulpit of today may have come from teaching methods in the seminary of yesterday. For any lack of authority in the pulpit now, we who have taught the ministers of today must bear much of the blame, especially those of us who have taught homiletics as a science and not as an art. Conversely, if the Church wishes to strengthen the pulpit of tomorrow, our leaders can find no surer way than to strengthen the seminary today, above all in the teaching of theology and homiletics. Meanwhile the pastor on the field may suffer as a scapegoat because of what we failed to teach him about the basis of authority in preaching. Here we consider only one aspect of the matter.

A study of the pulpit, in both the past and the present, would show that in the preaching of other days the Bible occupied a larger place than in most churches now. In those other times, with their "olden, golden glory," the man behind the Book spoke with an authority not his own. "Thus says the Lord!" In many churches today the pulpit contains no Bible, and the minister feels the need of none. On the other hand, without becoming Barthian in some respects, many of us agree with the following pronouncement. It comes from a wise and learned observer of church life and work of both yesterday and today:

Amazing as it is, the people in general still believe in the Bible, in spite of the painstaking efforts of thousands of ministers, Sunday by Sunday, throughout several generations, to convince them that it is not essentially different from any other book. . . . The Bible is still an authority for the people. If they do not read it, or if in reading they discover that they cannot read it with profit, it is because we have taught them that it is unscientific to make its words contemporaneous and apply them personally to ourselves.[3]

To inquire into the nature of biblical authority would lead to still another book, much more difficult to prepare.[4] On all these matters I hold a high theory, much like that of Maclaren, who believed what the Bible teaches and assumes about its own authority. Robertson and other expositors would have stated the truth differently. Without attempting to clear up all the mysteries and problems connected with revelation and inspiration, let us take for granted that the Bible still speaks with authority from God. If so, one way to strengthen the pulpit of tomorrow would be to guide the student of today into a larger and wiser use of Holy Scripture in his preaching. Let us assume that a young pastor carries out the general idea of the present book, year after year. How will his expository preaching affect the minister himself?

1. SPENDING THE MORNING IN STUDY

A worthy plan should help to transform the work of the study from drudgery into delight. After a young minister has determined his main objectives, and has learned how to handle his tools, he should find joy day after day in mastering some book of the Bible. In dealing with the Acts, for instance, he can enjoy at home a self-made "refresher course" that will lead

[3] See Walter Lowrie, *Our Concern with the Theology of Crisis* (Boston: Meador Press, 1932), p. 212.

[4] See A. Richardson and W. Schweitzer, eds., *Biblical Authority for Today* (Philadelphia: Westminster Press, 1952).

him to study early church history, the doctrine of the Holy Spirit, the Christian teaching about the Church, the spirit of apostolic preaching, the ideals in evangelism, the outreach of world missions, the problems of local church leadership, and various other matters of vital concern today. All of this is bound up in a single book of the Bible, a book with comparatively few difficulties for the man who has learned how to approach the Scriptures, and how to use scholarly works to help clear up any point of difficulty.

A wise pastor sets apart for Bible study an hour or more every morning, five days in the week, before he turns to anything else. He studies the Bible book at hand, first as a whole and then by paragraphs. Soon he begins to enjoy these hours of fellowship with the leaders of the Apostolic Church. Instead of seeing them as dim and shadowy figures far away, the "graduate student" gets to look on Peter and Paul, with other men of the Bible, as personal friends. Through them the pastor gains a new understanding of what it means to enjoy fellowship with the Living Christ, and to follow the guidance of the Holy Spirit. Herein lies no small part in "the romance of the ministry."

Let us suppose that a young pastor has been living for three or four months with the Book of Acts. He knows it as a whole, and he has worked his way through paragraph after paragraph. Often he has put a number of paragraphs together and studied them as a cluster; it may be in a chapter. After a while he comes to the account of Paul's work in Athens (Acts 17:16-34). The pastor knows that scholarly commentators speak of Paul as having failed in Athens, and of his changing over to another way of preaching (I Cor. 2:1-5) when he journeyed on to Corinth. The young man decides to study the matter for himself, as a homemade project. Of course he begins with the Bible record. What does he find?

The Apostle spent only a little while in Athens, whereas he labored in Corinth eighteen months and in Ephesus three years. In Athens he worked without a band of helpers, such as he had elsewhere. On Mars Hill he addressed a group of would-be philosophers eager for new sensations, and scornful of the gospel. In that sophisticated circle he began with a psychological approach unsurpassed in sermonic literature. Then he spoke about God the Creator and the Preserver. In like fashion our missionaries in the Far East have found it wise to begin with God the Father, rather than His Son. Because of this address, and perhaps other work in Athens, Paul won converts. The record does not state the number, which may have been five or six (Acts 17:34). After having served for years in two churches adjacent to state universities, I would not feel any sense of chagrin over this kind of results from a preaching mission. How many critics of Paul's preaching at Athens could have won more converts there? [5]

What has a study of the matter to do with preaching materials for next Sunday? Nothing. The experienced expositor does not live from hand to mouth. Neither does he keep hunting for preaching leads. He simply lets them come. After he has worked his way through a Bible book and has learned all that he wishes to know, he begins to use it in pasturing the flock. Meanwhile he can feed the sheep in some other Bible field that he has made ready. Some day, after he has completed a study of the Acts, he may wish to preach about "The Christian Idea of Brotherhood." At once he turns to a text dear to the heart of Dr. Albert Einstein and many other Jewish friends. God "hath made of one blood all nations of men, for to

---

[5] This paragraph owes much to J. M. English, "Elements of Persuasion in Paul's Address on Mars Hill," *Journal of American Theology*, Jan., 1896; and to D. J. Warneck, *Paulus im Lichte der heutigen Heidenmission* (Berlin, 1913).

dwell on the face of the earth" (17:26a, K.J.V.). Out of the surrounding paragraph the minister can draw the biblical materials for a sermon much needed today. As Paul showed in Athens, the brotherhood of man rests on the fatherhood of God, and this we believe because of what we know about Christ. Still the commentators, many of them, insist that Paul failed in Athens. Perhaps so, in the same sense that the Redeemer seemed to fail at Golgotha.

"Where can a young pastor find time for all of this book study of the Bible?" At first the difficulty may seem insurmountable. If a young man perseveres, however, and really masters the Book of the Acts, he will find that the plan later results in a saving of time. Pastor after pastor reports that he used to spend time and energy in casting about for sermon leads, and that he used to read up on a new unrelated subject almost every week. Seldom does such a man enjoy his hours of study. Why not? Partly because he scurries hither and thither through the Bible and other books. At the end of a year, or a lifetime, he wishes that he could have settled down to do more digging. Whenever a pastor begins doing that very thing, with the Bible at the heart of it all, he finds the hours of study an increasing delight.

"A beautiful theory! How does it work?" For practical answers turn to the lives of expositors in the past, and talk with such men of today. In almost every case you will find that the man who does effective expository work in the pulpit has learned to enjoy the work of the study. I cannot here testify without bias. Still I do not recall any effective expositor, past or present, who has not found delight in long morning hours alone with his Lord and the Book. On the other hand, I have had scores of letters from pastors, evidently men of character and ability, who have bewailed the lack of a plan for making the work of the study a source of increasing profit and joy. Here again, we who teach in the seminary must bear no small part of the blame. Instead of training young men to dig in the Bible and in other books, we have encouraged them to make sweeping "surveys." In most hands, like an old-fashioned Mother Hubbard dress, a survey sermon covers everything and touches nothing.

2. ENJOYING HOURS AMONG THE PEOPLE

The same principle of working biblically applies to pastoral care. For convenience the term here includes personal counseling. As Ruskin often insists, the heart has an instinct for its real duties. Any man called of God to serve as a pastor soon discovers that he learns to love whatever he does well, and that he does well what he has learned to love. "Love is the fulfilling of the law" (Rom. 13:10). The expository preacher, in the present sense of the term, needs to know the people and to enjoy the hours he devotes to the flock. Otherwise how could he use the Bible in meeting the needs of persons whom he did not know and love? To be frank, some of the best-known expositors have not excelled as pastors. Consequently they have contented themselves mainly with explaining the Scriptures. Almost without exception, those who have excelled in meeting human needs biblically have found delight in spending hours with people, often one by one.

Among all the galaxy of lecturers at Yale few have spoken with more insight and helpfulness than James Stalker. In the resulting volume he devotes the last four chapters to Paul as an ideal for a young pastor. Like his Lord, the Apostle excelled as a lover of men; he thought of them one by one, not en masse. Herein lies much of the secret in enjoying the "drudgery" of pastoral work. "See faces." In a moment of public confession, rare for a Scotsman, Stalker declared:

Almost any preacher, on reviewing a ministry of any considerable duration, would confess that his great mistake has been the neglect of individuals. . . . Not long ago, I had the opportunity, in passing from one charge to another, of reviewing a ministry of twelve years. The chief impression made upon me was that this was the point at which I had failed. I said to myself that henceforth I would write "individuals" on my heart as the watchword of my ministry.[6]

All of this and more a student of the Acts can learn from Paul, notably when he counsels with the elders from Ephesus (20:17-38). Here the Apostle opens up his heart and shows what it means to serve as a good pastor. If anyone wishes to deal with the passage as a whole, he can see in it a unity like that of a play with five parts. Here the Apostle lovingly takes "A Look Behind Him" (vss. 18-21), "A Look About Him" (vss. 22-27), "A Look Before Him" (vss. 28-32), "A Look Within Him" (vss. 33-35), and "A Look Above Him" (vss. 36-38). What an "apologia pro vita sua"!

In his lectures at Yale, Stalker spoke much about Paul as "A Man of Feeling." Like his Lord, the Apostle more than once gave way to tears, and that without shame. Hence he could inspire affection in the hearts of other strong men, an affection that led them to undying loyalty. Mighty as he became in matters of thought, Paul excelled even more in appealing to the heart. In the conversation with friends from Ephesus the Apostle shows the heart of a pastor in terms of love. Like John Watson, Phillips Brooks, Theodore L. Cuyler, Peter Ainslie, Maltbie D. Babcock, George W. Truett, and a host of other

[6] See *The Preacher and His Models* (London: Hodder & Stoughton, 1891), p. 229.

ministers now departed, the Apostle here reveals himself as:

I. A lover of Jesus Christ (vs. 19)
II. A lover of gospel preaching (vss. 20-21)
III. A lover of pastoral work (*idem*)
IV. A lover of the local church (vs. 28)
V. A lover of strong men (vss. 37-38)

Here lies the secret of effectiveness in an all-round pastoral ministry today. Love the people. For seventeen years our family enjoyed the pastoral oversight of a man who might have borne the name of Greatheart. Among the most difficult sort of parishioners—including "town and gown," with a seminary in between—the pastor loved everybody and everybody loved him. During all the years when one of us lived close to the heart of things in that church, we never saw a ripple on the surface of the waters. In almost every respect the work went forward from year to year. Changes came from time to time without any sign of dissent or displeasure. If anyone had asked this minister to quit working so hard as a pastor, he would have smiled and replied with Sir Wilfred Grenfell, "Don't pity me, I am having the time of my life."

"What has this to do with the work of the pulpit?" Much every way. Whenever that minister stood up to preach, he faced a church full of his friends, eager to drink in every word that fell from his lips. He loved them more than any other people on earth, and they loved him much as they loved the Lord. When he preached out of the Book, they heard him gladly because they had seen in him a present-day example of the gospel in action. So if any reader wishes to become an interpreter of the Bible in meeting the needs of men today, let him study Acts 20 in the light of some present-day example of what it means to be a good pastor.

3. TASTING THE JOYS OF THE PULPIT

"Nothing makes a preacher like preaching." True, and nothing unmakes a preacher so surely as doing sloppy work in the pulpit. If anyone wishes to become effective as a pulpit expositor, let him learn to do it well at length by doing it as well as he can each time. Whenever he prepares a message of this kind, let him hold it back until his own heart begins to burn. Then he can share this inner fire. By preparing and preaching heart-warming, soul-stirring sermons from the Bible anyone can learn more about this kind of pulpit work than by reading books on technique. Among all the foremost expositors of yesterday and today practically every one has learned at home by doing. By trial and error? No, not when a man relies on the Holy Spirit and follows His leading. By faith and with power, also with joy.

A novice in the difficult art cannot expect to produce a masterpiece every time he delivers an expository sermon. He may never do that once all the days of his life. Fortunately, it does not please God to advance His kingdom through masterpieces that call attention to themselves and their creators. According to Amiel, "Self must disappear when the Holy Spirit speaks, and when God acts." As the Apostle says, "We have this treasure in earthen vessels, to show that the transcendent power belongs to God and not to us" (II Cor. 4:7). Concerning a teaching minister the president of a university once told another layman: "Our pastor does not often soar to lofty heights, but he always feeds us well. He maintains a high average of pulpit performance."

This kind of expositor enjoys every minute in the pulpit. Suppose that he has been preaching here and there through the Acts. Now he comes to a case of conscience, a subject as delicate as it is difficult. According to Stalker, "He will never

be a preacher who does not know how to get at the conscience.
. . . We are preaching to the fancy, to the imagination, to intellect, to feeling, to will; but it is in the conscience that the battle is to be won or lost." [7] Instead of attempting to deal with the matter theoretically, or psychologically, the expositor takes up a Bible case, or it may be two contrasting cases. In the forefront of the sermon he reads Acts 24:10-27. Then he singles out the key verse, "Herein do I exercise myself, to have always a conscience void of offense toward God, and toward men" (vs. 16, K.J.V.).

A BIBLE STUDY IN CONSCIENCE

    I. Paul—the glory of a clean conscience
   II. Felix—the tragedy of an unclean conscience
  III. The Gospel—the secret of a clean conscience

In developing this last part one may have to look outside the passage, though not far. Elsewhere in the Acts one learns how Saul the persecutor became Paul the saint. First he had his conscience cleansed by Christ. Then Paul kept his conscience regulated every day. When Robert Murray McCheyne, saint of Scotland, lived in Dundee, his watch always showed the correct time. Whenever he left the city his watch did not tell the exact truth. In Dundee he passed by the church every day and unconsciously regulated his watch by the clock in the tower. Elsewhere he had no standard for telling the time.

Living close to Christ enables a believer to keep his conscience clean. The text suggests another way of keeping it in first-class trim. A wise man uses it. "I exercise myself." In the Greek this verb literally means to "work raw materials, to form, to practice, discipline, exercise." From the same root comes our word "ascetic." Like a set of muscles, or any other God-

[7] *Ibid.*, p. 156.

given power, the mysterious force that we know as conscience grows strong through proper use, or weak through lack of exercise. Think of poor Felix, with fatty degeneration of the conscience through lack of use. Only after the Almighty has wrought a miracle of grace can this kind of creature begin to have a clean conscience. The blood of Christ alone can "purify your conscience from dead works to serve the living God" (Heb. 9:14).[8]

After a man delivers a soul-searching sermon about conscience, he ought to feel a sense of abiding satisfaction. He has dealt with the heart needs of everyone present, and in the light of two Bible cases that everyone can see and understand. Better still, he has had an opportunity to apply the healing touch of Christ's dear hand to more than one soul in distress. During the week the minister will have conferences, one by one, with friends who long for peace of conscience and joy in the Holy Spirit. Who else in the community can taste such lasting joys as the man who enters the pulpit to deal with matters of conscience, and then leaves it to keep on ministering to "peace-parted souls," to "minds jangled, out of tune and harsh"?

The ability to preach heart-warming expository sermons grows with constant use of all one's God-given powers. Not every man called of God to preach can excel as an expositor. Not every useful minister has a teaching mind, shot through with imagination. But whenever a man of God feels drawn to this kind of pulpit work, he may safely assume that the impulse has come from above. He should also feel sure of increasing satisfaction as he grows in biblical knowledge and in Christian grace.

[8] For an interesting sermon, biblical but not expository, see Wm. M. Clow, *The Cross in Christian Experience* (London: Hodder & Stoughton, 1908), pp. 206-18, "The Cross and the Conscience"; also pp. 219-30.

4. HOLDING FELLOWSHIP WITH CHRIST

All of these satisfactions and delights come through faith, not merely through work. The preparation of any expository sermon worthy of the name calls for intellectual labor, which after a while ceases to seem like drudgery because it is being done in love. Morning hours in the study, later hours among the people, a crowning hour in the pulpit—all of these mean much or little, spiritually, according to the degree of a man's fellowship with Christ. In the study and elsewhere does the pastor abide with John Bunyan in "the house of the Interpreter"? Yes, if in the Bible a man discovers the Living Christ, and then introduces Him to others.

For a Bible study of fellowship with Christ throughout a career full of varied experiences look again at Paul. According to an able New Testament scholar the heart of the Apostle's life and work consisted in fellowship with the Living Christ, and not in doctrinal beliefs.[9] The sense of the present Living Christ dominates the climactic part of Acts 27. To students of literature this chapter affords the world's classic account of a storm at sea. To all believers in Christ the passage brings a message of hope for days of distress. At present let us think about vss. 23-25 in their setting. Let us assume that the "angel of God" means the Living Christ. "There stood by me this night the angel of God, whose I am, and whom I serve, saying, Fear not" (27:23-24 K.J.V.).

The Faith That Conquers Fear

Faith here means trusting the Living Christ.
I. Trusting Him amid the worst of storms
II. Trusting Him day after day
III. Trusting him for the sake of others.
IV. Trusting Him when the ship goes down

[9] See James S. Stewart, *A Man in Christ* (London: Hodder & Stoughton, 1947).

For examples of courage in the midst of a storm at sea turn to biography. Almost everyone knows about John Wesley's experience during a winter storm on the Atlantic. In October, 1735, at the age of thirty-two, he and others set sail for mission work in Georgia. On board that wooden sailing vessel he came to know and admire as his fellow passengers twenty-six Moravians. "When, at the close of a day's storm, an immense wave broke over the ship just as they were at their evening song, and the English passengers were screaming with terror at the prospect of immediate shipwreck, the Moravians continued their singing as calmly as if they had been in the chapel at Herrnhut." The day after the storm Wesley said to one of the Moravians, "Were you not afraid?"

"I thank God, no."

"But were not your women and children afraid?"

" 'No,' he answered mildly, 'our women and children are not afraid to die.' "

Soon after they went ashore at Savannah, Wesley sought out the local Moravian pastor to confer about the work that the younger men had come to do. Instead of talking about Wesley's mission the older man struck at the heart of something deeper. "Do you know Jesus Christ?" After Wesley had tried to answer this question, and a number of others equally searching, he decided that he did not know Christ as those Moravians knew Him. Two years later, on May 24, 1738, the founder of Methodism had a transforming experience.[10] From that time onward for almost fifty-three years he showed that the power and the joy of the ministry come from daily fellowship with the Living Lord.

To other leaders in the Church a sense of reality and the

---

[10] See Caleb T. Winchester, *The Life of John Wesley* (New York: The Macmillan Co., 1906), pp. 43-44, 57-58.

power of the Living Christ has come in various ways. As William James has made clear, such cases show "varieties of religious experience." Thomas Chalmers the Presbyterian, Dwight L. Moody the Congregationalist, and George W. Truett the Baptist illustrate this variety. Each of them engaged in full-time Christian service for a number of years before he became aware of what Paul meant by being "in Christ." Truett's experience deserves to become better known. One day this young pastor in Dallas went out hunting with a friend, Captain J. C. Arnold, chief of the city police, and a member of Truett's church. Accidentally the pastor's gun was discharged and Arnold was wounded. On the following Wednesday night, while people at the home church were praying for his recovery, Captain Arnold died.

All the rest of that week Truett went through Gethsemane. Again and again he told his wife that he could never again enter the pulpit and preach. She did not reproach him, but encouraged him to keep on praying and trusting the Lord for guidance. All that time they prayed together, not least for Mrs. Arnold. On Saturday night, after he had read much from the Bible, he fell asleep as he kept saying over and over, "My times are in Thy hands." Later that night Truett beheld a vision as real as that of Paul during the storm at sea.

There came a dream in which he saw Jesus as vividly and realistically as some earthly friend standing beside him. He heard the Master saying to him, "Be not afraid. You are my man from now on." He awoke. He waked his wife and told her. A second time he slept and the same vision and words were repeated. Again he told his wife what he had seen and heard. Again he slept, and again the Master came and spoke to him, just as before.[11]

[11] See Powhatan W. James, *George W. Truett: A Biography* (Rev. ed.; New York: The Macmillan Co., 1945), pp. 85-91.

"Be not afraid. You are my man from now on." In the strength of that vision Truett preached the next day, morning and evening, with spiritual power as never before. After that day he went on for almost fifty years of Christ-centered ministry. To others he may not seem to have excelled as an expositor, since this kind of preaching has not often found its way into his books of sermons. One week in Virginia he and I spoke from the same platform and ate at the same table. To the younger man those seven days showed anew the meaning of fellowship with Christ. One morning Truett spoke from II Kings 4, about the blessing of God on the Shunammite woman. Ever since that time I have enrolled Truett among my expository heroes.

Early in an even more amazing ministry young Spurgeon came to a crisis, different in detail but equally pronounced in its effect upon his later work for Christ.[12] With Spurgeon as with Truett, the transforming experience came at an hour when his entire ministerial future seemed to be hanging in the balance. With other men, such as Maclaren and Jowett, the decision to engage in a Christ-centered ministry seems to have come without any spectacular experience. However they reached the conclusion, all of these men would have agreed that in expository work, or in any other kind of preaching, power and joy come through a sense of the presence and blessing of the Living Christ.

5. LEARNING WHILE IN THE SEMINARY

How many of these expository joys can a young man experience while still in the seminary? Here we come into an area where opinions differ widely. Ideally, many of us professors believe that the seminary graduate ought to go out equipped to

---

[12] See *The Autobiography of Charles H. Spurgeon*, compiled by his wife and by his secretary, four large vols. (Chicago: Fleming H. Revell & Co., 1898), II, 192.

engage in a Bible-teaching ministry, and that he should know how to prepare popular expository sermons. Actually, we professors find it difficult to attain these ends in the time at our disposal. Where classes do not run large, some of us try to do with expository preaching what George Pierce Baker did with the drama in his "Workshop" at Harvard. In teaching a small group of men he did not rely mainly on lectures and assigned readings. He kept each student busy on a project. But after all our efforts we still meet former students who ask why we did not teach them how to prepare expository sermons. Such wonder we share, with sorrow.

This part of our task proves to be harder than it may seem from the other side of the teacher's desk. While in the seminary a young student with ability and promise may not have had enough experience of human nature, and enough knowledge of life, to know what hearers need today. Before he can hope to qualify as an expositor, he must know how men and women think and feel in times of sunshine and of shadow. As a rule this kind of pastoral experience must come gradually, through calling and through counseling. While the young pastor is gaining experience and insight, he may not feel ready to do expository work every Lord's Day. On the other hand, present-day methods of ministerial training should do much to remedy this lack of experience. The typical student of divinity today does not dwell all week in an ivory tower remote from human needs. In fact, his professors wish that he could take out of a busy life more hours for Bible study in the spirit of prayer.

Especially in the early part of his three-year course the student may not know enough about the Bible to use it as the main source of expository sermons. In three years, each of them consisting of only thirty weeks, a young man today attempts to master more than twice as many subjects as we older men studied in the seminary, where we had fewer outside attractions. Unless the student comes to the divinity school with a working knowledge of the Bible, how can he do much more than survey it in general and study certain parts intensively? Here again, present-day methods of planning the curriculum and of teaching the various subjects may do much to remedy the weaknesses of other days. Why should not every seminary begin now to plan for upper-class instruction in expository preaching? Meanwhile our seminary methods of teaching practical subjects lag far behind those in the medical schools of today. So do our facilities suffer by comparison.

Once more, the man in view may not have learned how to put things together in the way of synthesis. This calls for the use of constructive imagination. In college and in the first year or two at the seminary the student may have had practice only in taking things apart and in giving each fragment a label. Gradually he will learn to look at a psalm or a parable as a whole, and to deal with it as a unit of thought. Here, too, methods of teaching have been changing. The seminary student of tomorrow should gradually acquire the sort of synthesizing ability that distinguishes an educated minister from a wayside exhorter. Meanwhile we older men have growing confidence in the preachers of tomorrow, not least as biblical interpreters.

For all the shortcomings of seminary students and graduates in the past we professors must bear much of the blame. The effects of our teaching about the Bible and about sermons appear in a statement from one of the ablest graduate students with whom I have ever worked. Soon after he left a strong seminary he had an interview with a parishioner of middle age who had been trying to deepen her spiritual life. She had made a box full of little holes, and in each hole she had put a verse of Scripture, with no regard to the context. When in need of guidance she would draw out a slip at random and read it as a personal message from God. The young pastor told her that this method smacked of magic. "The Bible is not a book of charms and fetishes, with which you can conjure." Before he did his graduate work, the minister made an amazing discovery, which he is no doubt passing on to candidates for the ministry whom he now teaches in a Christian college.

It took me years to apply this lesson to myself. At last I began to see that I had employed much the same sort of magic. One Sunday I preached from Matthew, the next from Genesis, and a week later from I Peter. I played with the Bible much as she had played with her wooden box. I looked on Holy Scripture as a treasure store full of texts as unrelated as jewels in a box. At last I discovered that I ought to study and preach from the Bible the way it was written, a book at a time, with each verse in its own setting.[13]

This minister had for a while studied and preached as professors and books had led him to do. In the divinity school of tomorrow, let us hope, every student will begin to learn a "more excellent way." Some day, for instance, he will desire to make a special study of church leadership. As a living object lesson he may turn to the apostle Paul, in the classic chapter about a storm at sea. Undergirding the entire passage (Acts 27:1-44) runs the idea of faith as human weakness laying hold on divine power in time of need. "No man has any more religion than he can command in an emergency."

THE APOSTLE PAUL AS A LEADER OF MEN

I. In time of prosperity, caution (vss. 9-20)
II. In time of despair, optimism (vss. 21-26)
III. In time of crisis, resourcefulness (vss. 27-32)
IV. In time of confusion, action (vss. 33-38)
V. In time of waiting, perseverance (vs. 39-44)

[13] Statement prepared by request. Used by permission.

6. LOOKING FORWARD WITH ASSURANCE

A reading of this chapter and of this book ought to show that expository preaching worthy of the name blesses the pastor as well as the people. Largely because it enables him to meet their deepest needs, this way of working affords him satisfactions such as come to few of God's children here below. For many reasons, therefore, I hope that this book will help to encourage the ministers of tomorrow as they set their hearts on becoming able interpreters of God's Written Word. Like a teaching minister of old, let every prospective pastor "set his heart to study the law of the Lord, and to do it, and to teach his statutes and ordinances in Israel" (Ezra 7:10).

I hope that this book will do much to promote seminary work in expository preaching. To this kind of teaching I expect to devote the rest of my days, and I regret that I did too little of it in earlier years, when I was often busy about lesser things. I believe that the seminary exists mainly to prepare young men as pastors of local churches, as leaders in public prayer, and as preachers of God's Written Word. I hope that in the seminaries of tomorrow no graduate will have to start out blindly as an interpreter of God's Holy Book.

As with the medical school, or the engineering college, the seminary exists to guide the student in setting up lofty ideals for his lifework, in forming the right sort of working habits, and in determining to toil all his days as a master workman. There can be nothing new about these aims, but there ought to be new ways of putting them into the blood stream of the theological seminary. Let us plan so that every young "Timothy" of tomorrow will know how to respond to the appeal of a master teacher: "Do your best to present yourself to God as one approved, a workman who has no need to be ashamed, rightly handling the word of truth" (II Tim. 2:15).

In full view of all these ideals about training in the seminary I believe that expository preaching at its best must come from pastors on the field throughout the week. Even the ablest seminary graduate, with the best possible schooling, will become a still better interpreter of the Book as he grows more mature, and knows more about the hearts of the people. So I hope that this book will encourage many pastors to engage more largely in popular expository preaching, and to do it better week after week. Here I can only quote from the Book a portion of what it says about itself, and then close with a word of prayer. The Bible promise comes from the Gospel According to Isaiah, and from one of the noblest of all our evangelistic chapters:

As the rain and the snow come down from heaven,
  and return not thither but water the earth,
making it bring forth and sprout,
  giving seed to the sower and bread to the eater,
so shall my word be that goes forth from my mouth;
  it shall not return to me empty,
but it shall accomplish that which I purpose,
  and prosper in the thing for which I sent it.[14]

Blessed Lord, who hast caused all holy Scriptures to be written for our learning; Grant that we may in such wise hear them, read, mark, learn, and inwardly digest them, that by patience and comfort of thy holy Word, we may embrace, and ever hold fast, the blessed hope of everlasting life, which thou hast given us in our Saviour Jesus Christ. Amen.[15]

[14] Isa. 55:10-11.

[15] From *The Book of Common Prayer*, the Collect for the Second Sunday in Advent. See also the Epistle for the day, Rom. 15:4-13.

RELATED READINGS

CHAPTER I

THE WAYS OF EXPOSITORY PREACHERS

Baughman, Harry F. "Books on Biblical Preaching," *Interpretation*. Richmond, Virginia: October, 1950.

Blackwood, A. W. *Preaching from the Bible*. New York and Nashville: Abingdon Press, 1941.

Coggan, F. D. *The Man of the Word*. London: Canterbury Press, 1950.

Fosdick, Harry E. *The Modern Use of the Bible*. New York: The Macmillan Co., 1924. The "newer" view. Well written.

Knott, Harold E. *How to Prepare an Expository Sermon*. Cincinnati: Standard Publishing Co., 1930.

Maclaren, Alexander. *Expositions of Holy Scripture*. Grand Rapids: Wm. B. Eerdmans Publishing Co., 1937 (reprint).

Meyer, Frederick B. *Expository Preaching Plans and Methods*. New York: George H. Doran Co., 1912.

Morgan, G. Campbell. *Preaching*. New York: Fleming H. Revell Co., 1937.

CHAPTER II

THE GOALS IN EXPOSITORY PREACHING

Expository Times, The. Edinburgh: T. and T. Clark. Issued monthly since 1889.

Jeffs, H. *The Art of Exposition*. Boston: The Pilgrim Press, 1911.

Montgomery, R. Ames. *Expository Preaching*. New York: Fleming H. Revell Co., 1938.

Patton, Carl S. *The Use of the Bible in Preaching*. Chicago: Willett, Clark & Co., 1936. The "newer" view.

Ray, Jefferson D. *Expository Preaching*. Grand Rapids: Zondervan Publishing House, 1940.

Roach, Corwin C. *Preaching Values in the Bible*. Louisville: The Cloister Press, 1946.

Stevenson, Dwight E. *A Guide to Expository Preaching*. Lexington, Kentucky: College of the Bible, 1952. 10 pp., booklet.

Whitesell, Faris D. *The Art of Biblical Preaching*. Grand Rapids: Zondervan Publishing House, 1950.

CHAPTER III

THE SELECTION OF A BIBLE PASSAGE

Barnes, W. E. *The Psalms*, two vols., "Westminster Commentaries." London: Methuen & Co., Ltd., 1937.

Interpreter's Bible, The, Vol. IV. New York and Nashville: Abingdon Press. This volume, covering the Psalms and the Proverbs, is scheduled to appear in 1955.

Kirkpatrick, Alex F. *The Book of Psalms*, "Cambridge Bible." Cambridge: University Press, 1910.

Leslie, Elmer A. *The Psalms*. New York and Nashville: Abingdon Press, 1949.

Maclaren, Alex. *The Psalms, The Expositor's Bible*, six vols. Grand Rapids: Wm. B. Eerdmans Publishing Co. (reprint).

Meyer, Frederick B. *F. B. Meyer on the Psalms*. Grand Rapids: Zondervan Publishing House, 1952 (reprint).

Paterson, John. *The Praises of Israel*. New York: Charles Scribner's Sons, 1950.

Terrien, Samuel. *The Psalms and Their Meaning for Today*. Indianapolis: The Bobbs-Merrill Co., 1952.

Yates, Kyle M. *Preaching from the Psalms*. New York: Harper & Bros., 1948.

CHAPTER IV

THE GATHERING OF SERMON MATERIALS

Blackwood, A. W. *Preaching from Samuel*. New York and Nashville: Abingdon Press, 1946.

Blackwood, A. W. "The Minister's Filing System," *The Pulpit Digest*. Great Neck, New York, January, 1953.

Broadus, John A. *The Preparation and Delivery of Sermons*, rev. by J. B. Weatherspoon. New York: Harper & Bros., 1944.

Bryan, Dawson C. *The Art of Illustrating Sermons*. New York and Nashville: Abingdon Press, 1938.

Macleod, Donald, ed., *Here Is My Method,* a symposium. New York: Fleming H. Revell Co., 1952.

Sangster, W. E. *The Craft of Sermon Illustration*. Philadelphia: Westminster Press, 1950.

CHAPTER V

THE QUEST FOR THE UNIFYING TRUTH

Burney, Charles F. *The Book of Judges*. London, 1918.

Interpreter's Bible, The, Vol. II, Leviticus-Samuel. New York and Nashville: Abingdon Press, 1953.

Jones, Edgar DeWitt. *The Royalty of the Pulpit*. New York: Harper & Bros., 1951. A survey of the "Yale Lectures."

Jowett, John Henry. *The Preacher, His Life and Work*. New York: George H. Doran Co., 1912.

Phelps, Austin. *The Theory of Preaching* (abridged by F. D. Whitesell). Grand Rapids: Wm. A. Eerdmans Publishing Co., 1947.

CHAPTER VI

THE VARIETIES OF SERMON STRUCTURE

Bruce, A. B. *The Parabolic Teaching of Christ*. New York: George H. Doran Co., 1904.

Buttrick, George A. *The Parables of Jesus*. New York: Harper & Bros., 1928.

Cadoux, Arthur T. *The Parables of Jesus*. New York: The Macmillan Co., 1931.

Dodd, Charles H. *The Parables of the Kingdom*. New York: Charles Scribner's Sons, 1936.

Dods, Marcus. *The Parables of Our Lord,* two vols. London: Hodder & Stoughton, Ltd., n.d.

Interpreter's Bible, The, Vol. VII, Matthew-Mark. New York and Nashville: Abingdon Press, 1951.

Jülicher, D. Adolf, *Die Gleichnisreden Jesu*. Tübingen, 1910.

Manson, T. W. *The Teaching of Jesus*. Cambridge: University Press, 1935.

Smith, Charles F. W. *The Jesus of the Parables*. Philadelphia: Westminster Press, 1948.

Taylor, William M. *The Parables of Our Saviour.* New York: Harper & Bros., 1929. Sermons.

Trench, Richard C. *Notes on the Parables of Our Lord.* Grand Rapids: Baker Book House, 1948 (reprint).

CHAPTER VII

THE CONCERN ABOUT A FITTING STYLE

Blunt, A. W. F. *The Acts of the Apostles.* Oxford: The Clarendon Press, 1922.

Bruce, F. F. *The Acts of the Apostles.* London: Tyndale Press, 1951. Erudite; technical.

Chappell, Clovis G. *When the Church Was Young.* New York and Nashville: Abingdon Press, 1950. Sermons.

Dana, H. E. *The Holy Spirit in Acts.* Kansas City: Central Seminary Press, 1943.

Findlay, J. A. *The Acts of the Apostles.* London: Student Christian Movement Press, 1934.

Flesch, Rudolf. *The Art of Readable Writing.* New York: Harper & Bros., 1949. Secular.

Fowler, H. W. and F. G. *The King's English.* New York: Oxford University Press, third ed., 1931. Secular. Standard.

Interpreter's Bible, The, Vol. VIII, Luke-John. New York and Nashville: Abingdon Press, 1952.

Knowling, R. J. *The Acts of the Apostles,* "Expositor's Greek Testament." Grand Rapids: Wm. B. Eerdmans Publishing Co., n. d.

Lenski, R. C. H. *The Interpretation of the Acts of the Apostles.* Columbus, Ohio: Wartburg Press. 1934.

Luccock, Halford E. *The Acts of the Apostles in Present-Day Preaching.* Chicago: Willett, Clark & Co., 1942.

Quiller-Couch, Sir Arthur T. *On the Art of Writing.* New York: G. P. Putman's Sons, 1916.

Rackham, Richard B. *The Acts of the Apostles,* "Westminster Commentaries." London: Methuen & Co., Ltd., 1906. Recommended strongly.

Tittle, Ernest F. *The Gospel According to Luke.* New York: Harper & Bros., 1951.

CHAPTER VIII

THE CALL FOR A PLEASING DELIVERY

Curry, S. S. *The Vocal and Literary Interpretation of the Bible.* New York: The Macmillan Co., 1903.

Hegarty, Edward J. *Showmanship in Public Speaking.* New York: McGraw-Hill Book Co., 1952. Secular.

Kirkpatrick, Robert W. *The Creative Delivery of Sermons.* New York: The Macmillan Co., 1944.

Macartney, Clarence E. *Preaching Without Notes.* New York and Nashville: Abingdon Press, 1946. One chapter on the subject.

Parker, Everett C., et al. *Religious Radio.* New York: Harper & Bros., 1948. Bibliography.

Speer, Robert E. *How to Speak Effectively Without Notes.* New York: Fleming H. Revell Co., 1909.

Storrs, Richard S. *Conditions of Success in Preaching Without Notes.* New York: Dodd, Mead & Co., 1875.

CHAPTER IX

THE QUESTIONS FROM AN OPEN FORUM

Baughman, Harry F. *Preaching from the Propers.* Philadelphia: Muhlenberg Press, 1949.

Blackwood, A. W. *Planning a Year's Pulpit Work.* New York and Nashville: Abingdon Press, 1942.

Crossland, Weldon. *A Planned Program for the Church Year.* New York and Nashville: Abingdon Press, 1951.

Easton, B. S., and Robbins, H. C. *The Eternal Word in the Modern World.* New York: Charles Scribner's Sons, 1937. (*The Book of Common Prayer.*)

Gibson, George M. *The Story of the Christian Year.* New York and Nashville: Abingdon Press, 1945.

Jefferson, Charles E. *The Building of the Church.* New York: The Macmillan Co., 1910.

Lenski, R. C. H. *The Sermon: Its Homiletical Construction.* Columbus, Ohio: Lutheran Book Concern, 1927.

Ockenga, Harold J. *The Comfort of God.* New York: Fleming H. Revell Co., 1944. Sermons.

Scott, A. Boyd. *Preaching Week by Week.* London: Hodder & Stoughton, Ltd., 1929.

Seidenspinner, Clarence. *Great Protestant Festivals.* New York: Henry Schuman, 1952.

CHAPTER X
THE EFFECT UPON THE LOCAL PASTOR

Black, James. *The Mystery of Preaching.* New York: Fleming H. Revell Co., 1924.

Brown, Charles R. *The Art of Preaching.* New York: The Macmillan Co., 1922.

Calkins, Raymond. *The Romance of the Ministry.* Boston: Pilgrim Press, 1944.

Eberhardt, Charles R. *The Bible in the Making of Ministers: The Lifework of W. W. White.* New York: Association Press, 1949.

Guffin, Gilbert L. *Called of God: The Work of the Ministry.* New York: Fleming H. Revell Co., 1951.

Kuist, Howard T. *These Words Upon Thy Heart.* Richmond, Virginia: John Knox Press, 1947.

Love, Julian P. *How to Read the Bible.* New York: The Macmillan Co., 1940.

Oman, John. *Concerning the Ministry.* New York: Harper & Bros., 1937.

Spann, J. Richard, ed. *The Ministry.* New York and Nashville: Abingdon Press, 1949. A symposium.

Stewart, James S. *Heralds of God.* New York: Charles Scribner's Sons, 1946.

INDEX OF PASSAGES FOR PREACHING

WHAT TO PREACH

What we preach is not ourselves, but Jesus Christ as Lord, with ourselves as your servants for Jesus' sake. For it is the God who said, "Let light shine out of darkness," who has shone in our hearts to give the light of the knowledge of the glory of God in the face of Christ.

But we have this treasure in earthen vessels, to show that the transcendent power belongs to God and not to us. (II Cor. 4:5-7.)

INDEX OF PERSONS AND SUBJECTS

INDEX OF PERSONS AND SUBJECTS

INDEX OF PERSONS AND SUBJECTS